Table of Contents

Part One
Planning

Chapter 1 - What's the Big Deal?

Teamwork is a beautiful thing. Great teams are capable of producing something that an individual working alone could never do. If you've been lucky enough to be on a team that gels and works well together, you'll remember the warm, fuzzy feeling you had when everything clicked. It's hard to put your finger on what makes that moment happen, but the heartbeat of any team is controlled by the individuals who comprise it--each with their own strengths and weaknesses.

If you browse the web and most bookshelves today, you'll find loads of books about building teams and recruiting staff, but they all seem to be missing a few key parts of the equation. Where do you find talented staff? Once you've made a hire, how do you retain that person? How do you help him or her grow? All of these questions are important to answer if you want to build a strong team and ultimately a successful company.

If you've never been involved in hiring individuals before, the concept might seem like a simple one. Surely all that's involved is selecting a candidate with the appropriate skills and adding that person to the team! But it's not quite as simple as that. Competition for good talent is fierce, and hiring the wrong person can be detrimental in a team environment.

Let's face it: no one teaches you how to hire in high school, college, or even business school. This book aims to answer crucial questions and focus on all stages of recruitment, from attracting potential candidates right through to their retention and growth. In this first chapter, we'll take a general look at why people are the most important part of your business and why recruiting them can make such a big difference in your company. In particular, we'll focus on the different stages of recruiting and how they align with each of the chapters in this book.

Who this book is for

During my career, I've been involved in hundreds of interviews, including at

Google, Facebook, and other tech companies, and I've sat on both sides of the desk. Whether I was the interviewer or the interviewee, I always paid special attention to the process. Some candidates stood out from the crowd immediately, while others were just another resume in a million. I've seen great interviews with impressive candidates--and bad candidates struggling through even worse interviews.

Whether you're a seasoned CEO or a new manager looking to build a team, you face the same challenges: finding the best people for your company isn't an easy task. Following a few simple steps can make a huge difference between an average hiring experience and a great one. Hiring people is a fine art, and putting in some work to improve it will benefit you in the long run.

This book is written for anyone looking to build teams and grow talent-- entrepreneurs, founders, CEOs, or managers simply looking to grow their team. Regardless of your level of hiring experience, hiring is something that needs constant attention and focus, and the topics covered in this book will guide you along your hiring journey.

It's worth mentioning that the hiring experience will differ from person to person, but the topics and tips we'll cover here will help guide you as you embark on the worthy journey of growing and building your team.

The different stages of recruiting

At it's core, recruiting a new employee is divided into four key stages: planning, attracting, selecting, and retaining.

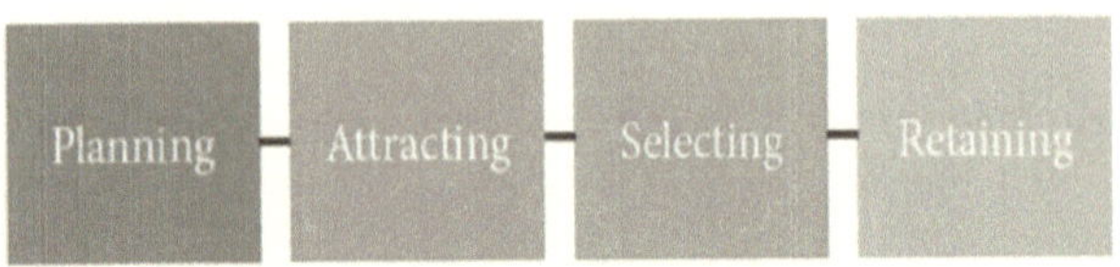

The four key stages of the recruitment process

Planning

In the planning stage of recruiting, it's important to understand what you're trying to build. When you're done recruiting, what will the team look like? What skills do you need to build your product? Before embarking on any project, planning is the key to success, so the planning phase means clearly defining the potential roles and responsibilities that you require.

Attracting

The attracting stage of recruitment deals with building a pipeline and attracting potential talent to your company, and to do this, it's important to understand why anyone would want to work for you. The truth is that successfully hiring great talent doesn't start from the minute that potential candidates attend an interview--it starts from the first time they come across your company. This could be through anything from your website to an advert to a fellow employee wearing your branding at a tech conference.

Selecting

Perhaps the most critical part of the recruitment process, the selection stage involves selecting the best candidate *for your company*. This isn't just about hiring the best candidate technically but rather the best candidate for your company. The skills and attributes needed for a role can vary from company to company, which is why the selection stage is very important.

Retaining

Once you've hired your epic employee, the last thing you want to do is to kick back and assume they'll stay with your company forever. In the modern environment, the reality is that most employees will start to seek greener pastures as soon as they aren't growing or having their needs fulfilled. I personally feel that the retention phase is the most important part in an employee's journey at your company. You've worked so hard to find this person and get them up to speed on your product, it's crucial that you don't lose them after you've invested so much in them.

How to read this book

There are individual chapters to help you through each stage of your recruitment process, with the idea of referring back to different sections depending on the stage of your process. This book isn't intended to be read front to back, like a novel--you can open any chapter and read it in a modular fashion. I hope it becomes your very best friend, a trusted ally as you begin to grow your team.

This book is divided into four key stages of the recruitment process-- planning, attracting, selecting, and retaining talent--and will guide you through each phase of your recruitment pipeline. I've mapped each of the chapters in the book according to the four key stages of recruiting.

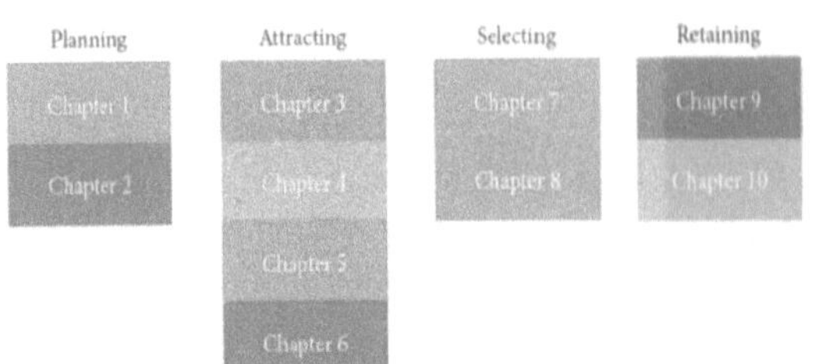

The chapters in this book are divided into four key stages of the recruitment process.

People are the most important part of your business

I've had the opportunity to work in all sorts of tech companies, right from large corporations to small startups. To me, one of the most intriguing tech environments is that of the startup. When you begin in a startup, there are so many things happening all at once. New product features, sales, customer management--managing all of these areas takes time, and all of them are key to building a solid company. But, crucially, while all of these things are important, none of them are actually possible without people. It reminds me of one of my favourite quotes from the book, *The Hard Thing about Hard Things*, by Ben Horowitz:

"We take care of the people, the products and the profits...in that order."

If you stop and analyse it for a second, it might seem a bit strange. To a new founder or a busy manager, hearing that you need to take care of your people and manage talent before adding new features to a product (or even getting it to market) might seem like the most counterintuitive thing you could possibly do. Surely, if there are no product features to build, there's nothing to sell! The reality is that having the wrong people in your company directly impacts your ability to create and deliver products. Without a winning product, you simply won't generate profits, which means the speedy end for a company that's just beginning to flourish.

Whether you're experienced at hiring people or brand new to it, you know in your heart of hearts that hiring people takes time. And if you're looking to hire the right people for your business, it can take even more time.

Large businesses and fledgling startups face similar challenges--hiring is tough on a small scale and even tougher on a large one. Not to mention the fact that it can become extremely frustrating when you're recruiting for a particular set of skills and attributes, the candidates you interview repeatedly miss the mark. For busy managers, interviewing repeatedly for the same role and not finding the perfect person feels like a complete and utter waste of time.

Competition is fierce

Fortunately, the good talent is out there! But you're up against some tough competition. Employees around the world are constantly bombarded with unsolicited emails from recruiters sending them exciting job offers with bigger and better salaries, and many of those employees take a look around their current office and opt to make that jump.

On top of this, it seems that there isn't enough new raw talent entering the marketplace. Dame Tessa Jowell recently stated the following about the technology sector in London, UK:

> *"With at least 25,000 new tech jobs in London every year ... just 2,400 students chose a technology-specific course."*

Considering the size of the technology sector in London, that's a staggering number. Not only is tech education not meeting the requirements of a growing industry, but due to talent shortage, salaries in the tech industry have started to skyrocket. If you take a look at the software industry in particular, the opportunity for software engineers to leapfrog between companies and make big jumps on the career ladder is becoming evident in resumes. Many software engineers stay at a company for a couple of years before moving on to the next higher paid job. Talent shortage and higher salaries also means that it's easier for your competition to poach your top talent.

What does this all mean?

If you want to hire the best people for your business, you need to invest the time and effort and put hiring first. I can't stress this enough: having the right people working on an already brilliant team can make a big difference to an already brilliant product.

The quality of the people and teams in your company is your most valuable resource. A business is the group of people who run it. It's not the logo, the brand, the website, or the product. Next time you conduct an interview, remember that the person opposite you could unlock a world of possibilities for your organisation.

Be realistic

As you read through this book, it's important to remember that there's no magic recipe when it comes to hiring. The process of finding the right people can't be rushed, and setting unrealistic goals will only serve to create stress and make the hiring process unpleasant.

I remember a few years ago I was sitting in front of the CEO of a company that I had been with for a few years. I was a newly appointed Head of Engineering, and as you can imagine, I was eager to impress. The company was on a big recruitment drive as we had just received a large amount of funding from our investors. As a department, we were tasked with hiring an extra 30 new team members with a mix of software engineers, quality assurance engineers, and product owners. According to the promises made to our investors, we were due to have these extra 30 employees recruited and contributing to the product within 3 months. Once fully hired, this would effectively double the size of our department. The CEO barked across the room at me,

"Why haven't we hired the full team yet? It's a simple equation; we have three months to get the team in place. You are behind and currently failing."

After 2 months, we had hired 20 of those new team members, but we still had another 10 to go. It's worth mentioning that hiring 20 team members in 2 months is a mammoth task achieved with a lot of dedication and teamwork from all departments involved! However, if you're driven purely by targets or haven't dealt closely with recruitment, an achievement like this can often be overlooked or misunderstood.

From a practical point of view, the CEO was correct: we had 30 new team members to hire, and we had only managed to hire 20 in the allotted time. If you looked at the hiring from a purely numbers point of view, we hadn't achieved our goal. However, the reality is that hiring people isn't quite the same as hiring a car. When you want to hire a car, you pick the make and model, pay your money, and drive away. As any experienced hiring manager will tell you, hiring people is a bit hit-and-miss and can't be compared to a simple transaction.

If you use the hiring a car mentality for hiring people, you'll have a tough road ahead of you. Recruitment is an ever changing landscape, and peaks and troughs in the market translate into wildly varying levels of candidate availability. Moreover, a big part of recruitment is about building relationships, which takes time.

Roll with the seasons

Seasonal factors also play a role in the market. You'll find that peaks in hiring correspond to holiday periods, with the big months being January to February and late September to October. Quite often, people come back from a long holiday period with a renewed mindset to make a job move. Bonus payouts and shares will also affect this. In the build up to these months, you might learn that finding potential candidates is difficult because they're holding out for a better time to leave their current company.

People will always come and go, and you might find that the specific person you want to hire is currently happily employed by another company. Timing is everything. You can aim to achieve a certain amount of hires within a time frame, but in reality, you'll have to adjust your mindset and accept in the fact that hiring takes time and effort. You might not be able to fill all of your vacancies in a given timeframe, or you might have to adjust your expectations and hire someone who isn't "perfect".

Start off small

Embarking on a large round of hiring can seem like a daunting task, so I find that it's often easiest to get started on a smaller scale. Think about one of the particular roles that you're hiring for and dial in your focus onto that role. It'll take time, but once you've made that initial hire, you'll find that it gets easier and easier. Much like any discipline, practice makes perfect, and recruiting people takes practice. With each new hire, you're one step closer to building a great team.

Even if you've never hired even one person before, remember that every organisation started with a first hire at some point.

Be prepared to play catch up

In addition to hiring new people, you have to be prepared for the fact that people working for your company will inevitably end up leaving and moving on to new jobs. If you're in the middle of a recruitment drive, this can be very frustrating as it feels like you're making two steps forward and one step back.

When you set out on a period of big hiring--or even when you don't--don't take it for granted that you won't lose anyone on your current staff. People are often averse to change, and new employees bring change with them. For employees who have been with the company for a longer period of time, this new period of flux can be unsettling. Be prepared for the possibility that you might lose members of your team, and take into account that this attrition might affect your hiring plan.

While you have your eyes on the prize and you're fully focused on hiring new people, it's important not to forget about your existing employees. After all, once you've made hires, the last thing you want to do is lose that talent due to neglect. We will be focussing on this in chapter 7.

Don't rush things

I've often seen senior managers place a high emphasis on hiring new staff within a certain time period. New employees are often seen as just another wheel in the cog, but the reality is that each and every one of them is equally important to the success of your business. Hiring with focus is important, but hiring for the sake of filling a role isn't the right path to go down.

As the deadline for hiring new employees begins to approach, crunch time begins, and the pressure to hire new staff starts to take its toll. With this added pressure comes the temptation to lower the bar and hire someone who doesn't quite fit the role. I have to admit, I've been guilty of this, but resist the urge, because it's the worst thing you can do. As we've already learned, people are the most important part of your business, and lowering the bar to fill a seat can affect the rest of the team. Remember that once you've made this hire, you might find yourself having to fire this person for underperforming. Hiring correctly in the first place could save you from an unavoidable situation.

The real solution

Speaking of firing, you may have heard the quote,

"Hire slow, fire fast".

While I don't entirely agree with this sentiment, you can see the logic. I truly believe that the best way to hire people is to do it slowly and with caution. But this isn't to say that you should drag out the hiring process and make the potential candidate wait a long time to receive a "yes" or "no" from your company. You want to carefully consider each candidate and commit the appropriate time to the recruitment process.

Recruiting too slowly for key positions can be a liability in a fast-paced industry, especially with fierce competition in the startup world, but it is more about the way you and your company treat people over longer periods of time that has a greater impact on your recruiting efforts.

The mantra "hire slow, fire fast" is especially important in the world of startups because they usually need to create a lean, product-building machine without unnecessary baggage. If you're a new startup in a fiercely competitive market, the last thing you need is people on your team who aren't driving you forward.

Summary

- People are the most important part of your business and can be the difference between a good product and a great one.
- There's no formula or recipe for success when it comes to hiring. Building great teams requires time and attention to detail, which will ultimately pay off in the long run.
- The demand for skilled talent in for both startups and established companies around the world is a constant challenge.
- Recruiting staff isn't the same as a simple, single transaction; seasonal changes and timing can play a big part in the frequency of your hires.
- Don't rush the process. Hiring with focus is important, but hiring for the sake of filling a role isn't the right path to go down.

Chapter 2 - Culture

In the modern startup world the competition for talent is fierce--if your organisation doesn't offer something that resonates with a potential candidate, reaching out to great talent can be tough. In most cases, cultural fit is a deciding factor, so in this chapter, we'll take a look at why culture plays such an important role in recruitment and what it means for your organisation. It's important to differentiate between *perks* and *culture*, and as we progress through this chapter, we'll define core values and why they're the key to hiring and maintaining great talent.

The all important question

"Is this an organisation where I would want to work?" This is the question that most potential employees ask themselves as they learn more about your organisation. From the minute they first interact with your website and have contact with you, they're forming an opinion of what it might be like to work for you.

Stop for a second and think about the office where you currently work. Think about the people, the values, and the mission of your organisation. Now imagine that you're a new employee visiting for the first time, and ask yourself, "Is this a place where I would want to work?" If the answer to your question is "Yes!", then we're off to a good start. If you hesitated for too long or the answer is "No!", then imagine what might be running through your candidate's head when he or she first comes into contact with your organisation. If you aren't completely certain that you would want to work in your company, you're going to have to go a long way to convince someone else to!

Your organisation's brand and culture are often the only things that a candidate might come into contact with before spending any actual physical time at your company. While you might not always be in the position to influence the culture of your company, it's important to understand the role that it plays in recruitment.

Culture is everything

There are so many different definitions for "culture" these days. If you scan the job descriptions of most startups, a trend emerges. These job descriptions are packed with perks and benefits to sound very appealing and to match what other startups are offering. Some of them sound like a great addition to the job, but never mistake perks for culture.

When many people hear the words "startup culture", they think of the stereotypes: craft beer Thursdays, free massage Fridays, and bring your dog to work Mondays. The word "culture" has become a misleading buzzword, but the Oxford Dictionary defines it as:

"The ideas, customs, and social behaviour of a particular people or society"

Let's break this down a little. In our context, the ideas of a culture are the beliefs and assumptions of an organisation--the customs and social behaviour are the stories, the events, the way people dress, and the layout of the office. If you put it all together, the culture of a startup is shaped by the collective beliefs and attitudes of the people in the company.

Regardless of whether you're in a position to influence your company's culture, the truth is that people want to work for companies with a great culture. When times get tough and money gets tight, perks start to disappear, but the culture of the company binds its people together. If you've ever been on an interview or visited the offices of a successful company, there's a palpable energy and excitement in the air. The people who work there are proud of their company, and you can sense it in the way they describe their work. It's no accident that strong culture produces successful companies--it includes the vision, the values, and the people.

The title of this chapter is a pretty bold one. Suggesting that culture is everything implies that it's the key aspect to the success of your organisation. Have you heard the saying, *"culture eats strategy for breakfast"*? It means that as your organisation begins to grow and scale, your long-term plan will only get you so far, but its culture will create a meaningful purpose and bond teams together to fight through the tough times.

It's true that there's a greater likelihood that employees will stay with an organisation when the work feels meaningful, which is why it's so important to consider your organisation's culture when you approach hiring. A classic since its publication in 1954, *The Practice of Management* was the first book to look at management as a whole and being a manager as a separate responsibility. In his book, Peter Drucker dedicates an entire chapter to what he called the "spirit of an organisation".

In this chapter, he writes:

"Management by objectives tells a manager what he ought to do. The proper organisation of his job enables him to do it. But it is the spirit of the organisation that determines whether he will do it. It is the spirit that motivates, that calls upon a man's reserves of dedication and effort, that decides whether he will give his best or do just enough to get by."

Culture plays such an important role in recruiting and the success of your organisation. In the end, it is the spirit of your organisation that matters more than anything.

Core values

So what is really important to the success of your organisation? The answer to that simple question is actually linked to the mission and core values of your organisation. Core values are the guiding principles or codes of conduct upon which a company was founded and operates under on a daily basis. Rather than these core values being vague ideas, they should be a real, daily part of the organisation and embodied. You may be familiar with the shoe company Zappos[1]. Its core values are communicated and given to each and every employee in an effort to help them drive the success of the organisation. For example, they list core values such as "deliver WOW through service", "embrace and drive change", and "do more with less" to name a few[2]. They use these core values as a part of the daily decisions that they make and every employee lives by them.

The important thing about core values is that they serve as the foundation on which tough company decisions are made. Let's use the search engine optimization company Moz[3] as an example--it openly displays core values on its website and attempts to have its employees, from top to bottom, live by them. The company has an acronym for its core, TAGFEE, which stands for Transparent, Authentic, Generous, Fun, Empathetic, and Exceptional. These core values are clearly and proudly displayed on the website with the clever use of graphics, making it fun to read at the same time.

Moz proudly displays its core values on its website's careers pages and in all job descriptions

While these core values are specific to Moz as an organisation, they play a key role in everything the company does. If you browse the careers section of its website, you'll easily spot those core values, as well as any job descriptions.

Every startup has different core values that ultimately drive its mission and success, and it's important to understand the pivotal role they play in recruiting. While yours might not be the same as Zappos, or Moz's, ensuring that those values are embedded in the hiring process can make a big difference in the calibre of people that you end up hiring. Once your core values are firmly established, the people you hire can continue to promote those values and ultimately drive the success of your organisation. Being open and transparent about your core values also means that every candidate who walks through your doors understands exactly what you're *really* about. Translation? If their values match yours, it saves you a mismatch right from the start.

Hiring for cultural fit

When times get tough and you're fighting for the success of your organisation, you want to be sure that the people around you all share the same core values and are all aiming for the same goal. One way to ensure that the people around you believe in the same vision is to ensure that you hire for cultural fit. I like the way that Brad Feld, Managing Director at the Foundry Group, puts it[4]:

> *"Every startup is going to have a company culture, by design or by default, so you might as well design yours with values that attract and keep the best possible talent. Once you've distinguished between your values and your vibe, hiring for cultural fit won't just be easier; it will give you better, and likely more diverse, employees."*

In an enjoyable working environment, positive energy starts to snowball throughout the company. We spend such a large part of our adult lives working with the people around us, so we want to create an environment where people want to work.

A good example of hiring for cultural fit is Palantir. As an organisation, it makes analysis platforms aimed at governmental clients. The founders knew from the start that they wanted to create products for enterprise organisations, which they knew would take a long time, and they needed brilliant people. Right from day one, they knew that they would need to hire wisely and conscientiously. Stephen Cohen, the co-founder of Palantir[5], says:

> *"That early understanding reflected the three salient properties that inhere in good company culture. First, a company must have very talented people. Second, they must have a long-term time orientation. Third, there must be what might be called a generative spirit, where people are constantly creating. With this framework, hiring is more understandable: you just find people who have or contribute to all three properties. Culture is the superstructure to choose and channel people's energies in the right direction."*

The benefits of hiring for cultural fit are endless. It's the glue that holds an organisation together, and when you hire people who fit with the culture, there's a greater likelihood that they'll want to stay.

Embed cultural fit into your hiring process

From the very first moment that a potential candidate comes into contact with your company, he or she begins to build an idea of what your organisation is all about. What does this company believe in? What are its values and mission? Which is why it is important to clearly communicate this message.

If you have this clearly defined from the start, it helps filter out candidates who aren't a good fit and will save you time in the long run. Any public-facing material should be aligned and clearly communicate company culture.

As you begin to conduct face-to-face interviews with candidates, the interview can be a great opportunity to learn more about them and *their* values. What motivates this person? What does he or she care about? Asking questions such as "What are you most proud of?", "What type of culture do you thrive in?", "How would you describe our culture based on what you've seen?", "Is this something that works for you?", and "What are you looking for?" are just a few examples of questions that allow you to find out more about the person's core beliefs. When interviewing, it's worth going a little further and finding out if the person is actually interested in the same industry as your organisation. For example, if your organisation is involved in the sports industry, it might be worth determining if the person you're interviewing is actually interested in sports. Establishing why someone wants to work in the same industry can help you understand if the applicant is truly interested in the values of your organisation or just looking to make a quick buck. Questions such as "What do you like about this company?" or "Why do you want to work here?" help you understand whether the candidate is sincerely interested in the job and if he or she will be motivated to perform if hired.

A huge part of our adult lives are spent at work with our colleagues, and when deciding if you should hire a person, it's worth asking whether this person will ultimately contribute to the success of the organisation--in terms of both product delivery and what he or she contributes to the overall office culture. Once you begin to align your hiring practices with the core culture of your company, you'll find that it becomes easier to screen potential candidates for a cultural fit. When there's harmony between the individual and the company culture, there will be a greater likelihood that the person will feel connected and want to stay. If you assess cultural fit throughout the recruiting process, you'll hire professionals who will thrive in their new roles, drive the success of your organisation, and ultimately save you time and money.

Summary

- Your organisation's brand and culture are often the only things that a candidate comes into contact with before spending any actual physical time with your company.
- Having clearly defined core values will help filter out candidates who aren't a good fit and will save you time in the long run.
- As the saying goes, "culture eats strategy for breakfast", and when times start to get tough, your core values are what really binds your teams together.
- The core values of your organisation are the guiding principles or codes of conduct upon which it was founded and operates under on a daily basis.
- Hiring employees who positively contribute to a company's culture helps foster a great working environment.
- By embedding cultural fit into your hiring process, you'll ensure that whether your organisation involves 10 people or 200 people, you're able to scale the core beliefs and values you set out right from the start.

References

1. Zappos - About Zappos Culture - http://www.zappos.com/d/about-zappos-culture
2. Zappos - Core Values - http://deliveringhappiness.com/book/zappos-core-values
3. Moz Website - http://moz.com

4. Brad Feld - Dilbert on Cultural Fit - http://www.feld.com/archives/2013/08/dilbert-on-cultural-fit.html
5. Blake Masters - Peter Thiel's CS183: Startup - Class 5 Notes Essay - http://www.feld.com/archives/2013/08/dilbert-on-cultural-fit.html

Part Two
Attracting

Chapter 3 - Inbound Recruiting

In this chapter we'll take a closer look at inbound recruiting, which involves spending time creating content, building brand awareness, and promoting your organisation to build relationships with future candidates. You'll learn why inbound recruiting is important even when you aren't currently hiring. We'll also look at how you can leverage your company's brand to generate interest for the different roles that you may be recruiting for and how you can track, analyse, and benefit from them. By the end of the chapter you'll be able to build and utilise a list of recruiting channels to promote all the roles that your company has to offer.

When you sell a product to potential customers through online marketing techniques, you might use different channels such as search engine optimisation (SEO), social media, or your own website. When you search for potential employees, it's important to think of the hiring process in the same way: the flow and decision logic is very similar, and, ultimately, you want to entice curious candidates (customers) into exploring the roles you have on offer (products) and then encourage them to apply for the role (buy that product).

From the very first moment a candidate comes into contact with your company, he or she is building an impression of your brand and culture. Your goal is to create a hiring experience for the candidate that this person will remember right up to the minute he or she starts working for you on his or her first day. Inbound recruiting focuses on building relationships with future candidates--it's about being visible in as many useful places as possible for the times when people may go looking for you.

The idea of treating potential candidates like customers is a shift from the traditional mindset of hiring. One of the mistakes inexperienced managers often make is to neglect the fact that the hiring process is not only about the candidate selling himself or herself to you, but also of you convincing the candidate that your company is worth working for!

Cost-effective hiring strategies

In the early days of a startup, money is tight and the idea of spending it on recruitment might be a tough one to make, but it doesn't have to be this way. Using a little creative flair, you'll find that there are actually a lot of different channels you can use to promote and generate awareness about recruitment in your company that are free or cost very little.

Using different channels to attract talent can help you reach candidates that you might not have reached using traditional methods. The reality is that the perfect candidates aren't looking for a job right now. They could be very happy in their current role and haven't considered moving on. This is where the concept of brand awareness comes in. Using different recruitment channels allows you to subtly keep your organisation in the back of a candidate's mind. It may simply be curiosity that leads them to look at your website and explore further.

By adopting different recruitment channels such as social media, your company website, or internal referrals, you'll slowly start to grow and build a pipeline of potential candidates. Building your brand enables you to hire amazing people and build a scalable hiring machine. Regardless of the size of your company, the concept of building brand awareness around your company and encouraging hiring should be a continuous one.

Using traditional channels for hiring, such as external recruiters, can be an expensive path to go down. While no hire is really a "free" hire due to the cost of time and effort, the pipeline that you will build around inbound recruiting will save you time and money in the long run. In chapter 9, we will look at the *real* cost of hiring a new employee, and it will soon become apparent how much money you can save using inbound recruitment as a cheaper option.

This isn't to say that you should only use inbound recruiting to hire employees. Depending on the size and growth of your company, recruiters can use these techniques in tandem--to hire the best people, you have to use every tool to sell your company!

Hiring even when you aren't hiring

As we discussed in chapter 1, recruiting new employees can be a roller coaster ride. There are many ups and downs in hiring frequency, and factors such as seasonal changes can affect your ability to make hires on a regular basis.

Even if you aren't currently hiring, it's always best to keep your recruiting options open. You never know who might be browsing your site, looking for a new role. If potential employees stop by and see that nothing's open, they'll immediately move on to another site without giving you another thought.

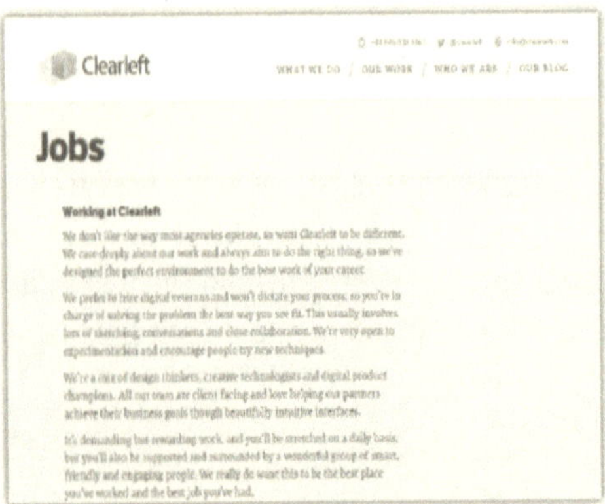

Clearleft actively shows that it's open to interested candidates even if it isn't currently hiring for a specific role. Source: clearleft.com

By maintaining an "always open" approach, you'll find that you occasionally receive resumes from candidates, ensuring that you constantly have a pipeline of people to contact when you do start hiring again. Who knows, you might just be able to squeeze the budget if the right candidate comes along!

Create a great careers website

As visitors to your website browse through your content, they're beginning to build a picture in their minds of what your brand is all about.

Potential candidates are using your site as a gauge for the culture and what they might expect if they work at your company. Your company website is the first port of call for interested candidates, which is why it's so important to leave a great impression right from the first visit.

Although dedicating a part of your website to recruitment might seem like an obvious thing to do, many sites simply list their open roles and don't place any special importance on this area of the site. A careers page on your website is a great way to be creative and really sell your brand and culture. Candidates are interested in learning more about your company and getting a feel for what it's like to work for you.

Many startups already use creative ideas on their careers page to promote the people who work for them and explain what the office is like. The Just Eat website does a great job of using photos of employees and testimonials to boost this area.

The Just Eat website gives a fun insight into what it's like to work there, while also showing its core values and culture. Source: careers.just-eat.com

When candidates visit your careers section, you want to thrill them and make them wish they had the opportunity to work at your company. Taking the time and effort to create a great careers section can go a long way in convincing potential employees to join you.

Making inbound recruiting fun

Inbound recruiting can seem like a tedious and serious task--there's constant work to do in terms of maintaining a public presence, being active on social media, and tracking your "conversions". But there's no reason why it can't be fun at the same time. With a few simple tricks, you can showcase your company's culture and add a little humour at the same time.

Hidden website messages

One of my favourite methods of promoting hiring is the hidden messages in websites. These messages aren't immediately visible and are aimed at developers or advanced users who might be looking deeper at the code behind your website.

Simple hidden messages are useful when recruiting software engineers.

Many technology companies have this message hidden in their websites to attract curious software engineers--for example, Microsoft, Flickr, Mozilla, Etsy, and SoundCloud all have recruitment messages hidden in their code.

Admittedly, this might only make its way in front of advanced users and software developers, but it's a fun way to showcase some of the talent on your own team and adds a bit of humour at the same time. Who knows who might stumble upon it!

Recruitment videos

Having a careers section on your company's website is a useful tool for many reasons, but in a world where almost every other company has that same section, it's hard to stand out. A few companies, such as Shopify, and Zendesk, go the extra mile by showcasing what they're all about using creative techniques such as recruitment videos.

If you want to show prospective employees what your company and people are really about, why not create a recruitment video? The tone can reflect your culture and let you literally, visually showcase the people and office environment.

The Shopify recruitment video is visually appealing and showcases the office environment with a touch of humour.

Creating a recruitment video costs less than you might think. With a little bit of camera hardware and editing software, you can create a video with the team for little more than the cost of your time. If you prefer to go down a more professional route, many video production companies can film and edit your video instead.

Another great thing about using videos is that they're shareable. At the time of writing this, the Dropbox recruitment video has had over 70K views!

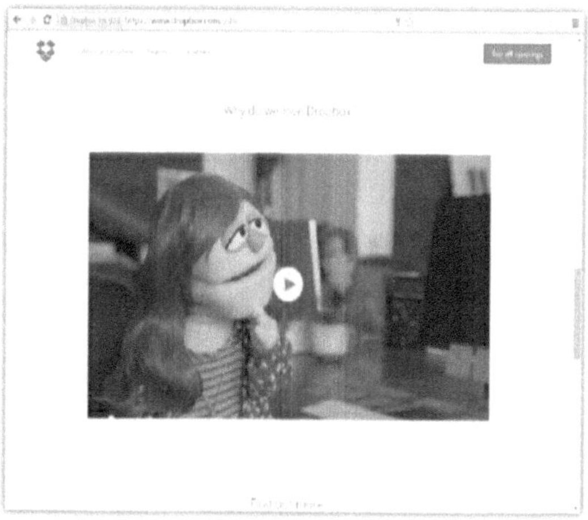

The Dropbox recruitment video uses puppets to showcase the company's humour and culture. Source: dropbox.com/jobs

In today's world, traditional approaches aren't enough to maintain a competitive advantage. You have to take advantage of every multimedia opportunity available to you.

Team blogs

If you look at websites for many of today's top startup companies, you might notice that they all have a team blog. These blogs can be used to proudly display what those teams are currently working on.

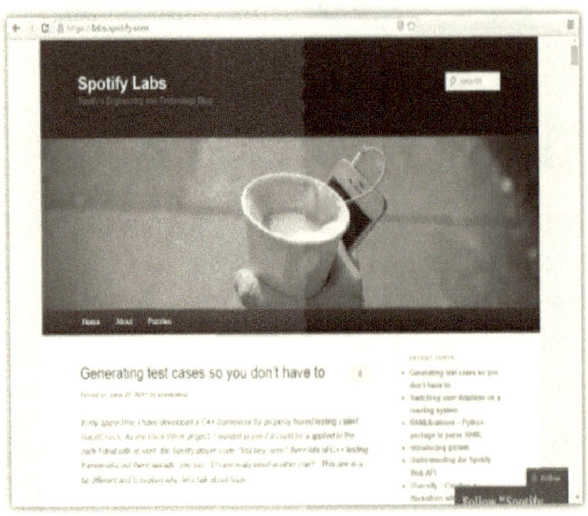

The Spotify tech team uses a blog to reach out to other people interested in technology.
Source: labs.spotify.com

A team blog doesn't have to follow a standard blog format; it can be used to talk about new features and releases or even a few of the daily challenges that the teams face. Every new piece of content created helps drive and boost SEO for your company. A team blog is a great example of inbound recruiting.

Setting up a team blog need not be complex as there are many different blogging engines out there that you can use to get started. Some of my favourite examples of current team blogs include *labs.spotify.com, shopify.com/technology, engineering.pinterest.com,* and *moz.com/devblog,* if you need some inspiration.

One of the important things to keep in mind is that a company blog that isn't updated regularly can quickly become a barren landscape that gives a terrible impression to interested visitors to your site. Assigning an owner or someone responsible for ensuring the site is updated on a regular basis is key to maintaining freshness. Encourage all members of your team to contribute, and you'll quickly find that the site begins to grow. I also recommend scheduling and staggering blog posts instead of publishing several all at once.

Social media

In the same way that you would use social media to sell and promote your product to customers, these platforms can be a great way to broadcast that you're hiring. Let's take the SEO company Moz as an example. As a Twitter user, I follow the Moz account because I love its product and think it's a great tool for SEO purposes. I might not be looking to move jobs, but as I'm reading my feed, something like this might pop up.

Social media can be a great place to attract talent.

Many technology companies have this message hidden in their websites to attract curious software engineers--for example, Microsoft, Flickr, Mozilla, Etsy, and SoundCloud all have recruitment messages hidden in their code.

Admittedly, this might only make its way in front of advanced users and software developers, but it's a fun way to showcase some of the talent on your own team and adds a bit of humour at the same time. Who knows who might stumble upon it!

Open source/side projects

Your employees might have side projects that closely relate to your product and industry. For example, I've worked in tech startups where many of my coworkers had side projects on open source projects or contributed to open source software.

If your company is in the tech sector and employs software engineers, side projects and open source projects can be an easy source of inbound recruiting. Adding a simple email address or a link to your careers page can be a great way for inquisitive engineers to learn more about your company.

Side projects don't just have to extend to open source software projects, though. You might have employees who work in a variety of different side projects, and if they're willing, they might generate interest for a role from an alternate source that you might never have thought of.

Tracking conversions

As user's progress through the flow of your careers page, there are opportunities to analyse different stages of the website funnel. By installing tracking snippets and using analytics tools such as Google Analytics, Mixpanel, or any other web analytics service, you'll be able to assess how people come to your site and which channels deliver the best results.

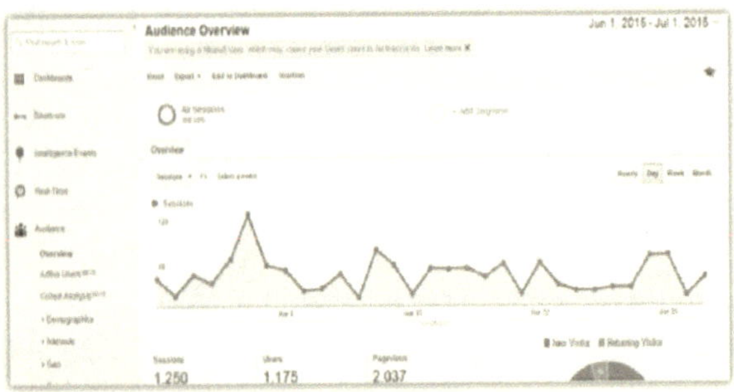

Web analytics products such as Google Analytics help track and measure website engagement. Source: google.com/analytics

By using analytics to track visitors to your website, you'll be able to improve and adjust certain aspects of it. With this knowledge, you can implement conversion rate optimization techniques that improve the number of people who read through a job description, fill in an application, and submit it.

Without analytics, you could be focusing your efforts in the wrong places. For example, if the majority of your candidates are coming through social media channels instead of directly through your website, it would make sense to focus your efforts on social media. Treating candidates as customers involves tracking their usage as well as optimising your efforts accordingly.

Recruiting is time-consuming, and the last thing you want to do is waste money by using the wrong tactics.

Going offline

Reaching out to potential candidates doesn't have to only involve online methods. Social connections, friends, corporate events, and even graduate fairs can be great sources of candidates for your recruitment pipeline.

There may be times when you feel like you've exhausted all avenues when it comes to hiring. You've broadcasted the role to social media sites and contacted potential candidates, but nothing seems to be working. When the deadline for building a team is approaching, the pipeline might feel more like it's dripping than gushing.

In the fantastic book *The Lean Startup*, Eric Ries discusses principles from lean manufacturing and agile development to improve the process of innovation. One is "getting out of the office", which describes how founders should seek alternate ways to build their product and speak to their customers instead of assuming what they want. The same principle applies to recruitment. Often the best sources can be found offline, simply by attending events and chatting to potential candidates.

Recruitment events

Often seen as more traditional, recruitment events are still a useful source of candidates. They aren't necessarily free, but for a small fee, you might reach a larger audience in a face-to-face setting than you would using online techniques. In addition, by meeting and chatting with you, candidates are more likely to remember you and your company.

Face-to-face time with interested candidates is underrated in more ways than one. Being able to talk with the founders of a company can be a great selling point when compared to online platforms or middleman recruiters. These events also give you the opportunity to advertise your company and give away free gear. At some of the larger ones, you can see an entire room of people walking around promoting your brand for you!

The landscape is evolving to match the requirements of employees around the world. Events such as HackerX and Silicon Milkroundabout operate slightly differently than the more traditional recruitment events, and depending on your target audience, you might find candidates that meet a specific set of criteria here. By attending a mix of different recruitment events, you'll be surprised at the different candidates who can help grow your recruitment pipeline.

Even if you aren't currently recruiting, sponsoring a local event can have an impact on your pipeline, too. Moving away from the traditional hiring mould means breaking out of the things that every other company is doing. The different techniques you use don't have to necessarily be earth shattering--something as simple as looking for different recruitment avenues can be a source of great candidates.

Graduate events

Graduates can be a great way to breathe new life into a team. As well as being eager to learn, they also introduce a level of diversity. Working with graduates has been a great experience for me personally, and many of those I've worked with have all grown into fantastic engineers who've gone on to lead teams of their own.

Universities around the world offer a variety of free recruitment events that you can use to hire graduates. The format differs from place to place, but they can be a great chance to speak to potential candidates and spread the word about your company. Who knows, even if they aren't right for you now, they might be in a few years' time--not to mention the fact that they could become potential paying customers for your product.

These events often allow you to take along banners or give away swag. Having young graduates walking around advertising your brand for free is a good thing! But it's a two-way street in lots of ways--they can offer your team many benefits.

Graduate events give you the opportunity to spend some face-to-face time with potential candidates.
Source: Jason Cartwright flickr.com/photos/jasoncartwright

Diversity

Graduates come from a variety of different backgrounds, and a fast-learning one from outside of your usual demographic can be a great way to introduce diversity on the team. Bringing young talent into your company creates a culture of mentoring that allows more senior people to grow as well.

Blank canvas

Fresh-faced graduates are often seen as a "blank canvas" when it comes to learning new things and ways of working. This gives you an opportunity to help them learn, grow, and become a part of your culture. Graduates have developed a habit for learning so they often seek to continuously learn in the working environment.

Increased competition

Due to their enthusiasm for learning and new work, graduates can add a healthy level of competition within a team, which in turn increases efficiency and productivity. Hiring graduates can be a great way to boost the skills, energy, and competitiveness on your teams.

Local meetups

If your company is involved in a particular market or uses certain technologies to build your product, you can be certain that there's a local meetup or community to match it. For example, if your product is for the fitness market, attending a fitness meetup in your local area is the perfect opportunity to spread word about your product and find like-minded individuals. Not to mention the fact that you could learn about your competition!

If your company employs software engineers, software testers, or product managers, attending the appropriate software meetups is a good way to spread the word about your company and generate interest among potential candidates. Getting involved in the local community is another good way to stay in touch with your particular market while still generating potential recruitment leads. If your employees attend these events and give presentations, they can be shining examples of what it's like to work for you and the different technologies that you might use. Give them the time and space to attend and present at local meetups--it will only benefit you in the long run!

There are several online websites that let you find local groups near you. Some of the more well-known ones include meetup.com and eventbrite.com, but for more specialized markets, you might need to search for niche websites.

Try not to attend only when you are hiring, but instead show an active interest and attend events continuously. Only attending when you're looking to hire will quickly become apparent, and regulars at these meetups will quickly be able to see through this!

Your employees are your best recruiters

A great source of untapped recruiting potential can be found within your very own company--your employees have a wide circle of influence and could be connected to some very talented individuals. A potential candidate might be much more open to chatting to you if they're given a reference from a friend.

Many companies already offer incentives for referrals from their own employees. Offering a simple cash reward or other incentive costs less than you think. As we will find out in the next chapter, hiring a new employee often costs more than the immediately visible costs, so save money where you can!

At first glance, offering recruitment incentives to your employees might seem expensive, but incentives are small in comparison to the fees that you might pay an external recruiter.

Many companies are already using this technique to find and source talented employees. After all, good talent knows good talent. Using referral incentives for hiring leads gives your employees the chance to make a little extra cash and helps you hire candidates who have references from your most reliable source--your current employees.

Summary

- It's important to be seen as hiring even when you aren't. By maintaining an "always open" approach, you'll find you constantly have a healthy pipeline of interested candidates.
- From the moment a candidate comes into contact with your company he or she will be building an impression about your brand and culture.
- Inbound recruiting involves using different channels such as social media, your website, and employee referrals.
- Inbound recruiting can be fun! Recruitment videos, hidden website messages, and team blogs are a few examples of methods at your disposal.
- Look to hire graduates as they are eager to learn and can be a great way to introduce diversity into your organisation.
- Your employees can be your best recruiters!

Chapter 4 - Planning for Hiring

Up to this point, we've been looking at why people are the most important part of your business. We've also talked about how the culture of your company will ultimately shape its future. But now it's time to get down to business: How do you actually build and grow your teams?

In this chapter, we'll dive into planning for recruitment and how to define the roles and responsibilities for the positions within your organisation. The first step should always start with planning.

What are you looking for? What sizes are your teams? What skills do you need? By the end of the chapter, you'll have a clear understanding about how to plan for a round of hiring as well as be able to create job descriptions that will appeal to potential candidates.

What are you looking for?

Whether you're hiring one or ten new employees, the process can seem daunting. Let's break down each stage of the hiring process into smaller chunks--handling a new round of recruitment can seem a lot easier when you're dealing with bite-sized pieces. In this chapter, we'll look at how to best approach the planning phase of recruitment.

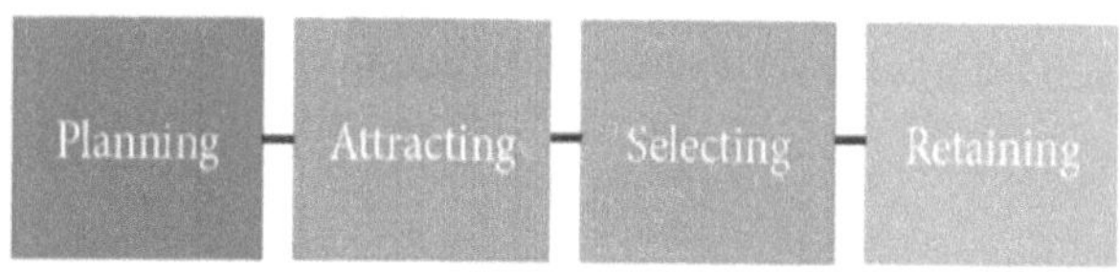

The four key stages of the recruitment process.

When you approach a round of hiring, no matter how big or small, planning is key to its success. Factors such as time frame, budget, and project requirements all affect the outcome of hiring. As we progress through this chapter, we'll look at how you can break down those three factors of hiring into smaller pieces to help you clearly understand your hiring goals and ambitions.

Understanding your organisation

It's important to have a clear idea about how your teams should be structured in order to make the hiring process as smooth as possible. I personally find that using something as simple as the classic organisational chart can be the best way to do it. An org chart shows you how people connect, communicate, and collaborate at work. You may already be familiar with the idea, but the most basic form is a diagram that shows the structure of an organisation and the relationships and relative ranks of its parts and positions/jobs.

Let's say for example that I was looking to expand my team by one new hire. The organisational chart for that team might look a little something like the image below.

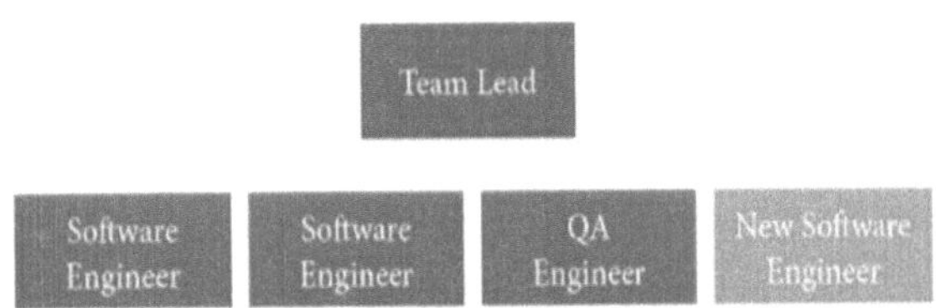

An organisational chart for a small team. The green square indicates a new hire to be made.

Although this image represents a small team in a much larger organisation, it helps to break down and highlight which new roles are being hired. If we take the team above and look at it in the context of the wider organisation, it might look a little something like the image below.

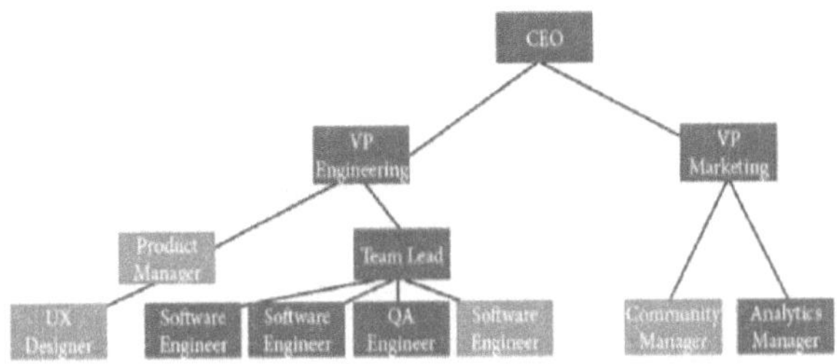

An organisational chart for a small organisation. The green squares indicate the new hires to be made.

When you're faced with hiring several large teams, these charts are excellent for breaking down each team into the "components" of the larger company. I personally prefer looking at org charts instead of long lists of names with no relation to each other. You can easily create an org chart using Excel or PowerPoint; distributing it among hiring managers puts you all on the same page about your organisation's teams and where the different roles fit in.

The next time you embark on a round of hiring, start with an org chart to get a clear picture of the roles that will ultimately make up your hiring strategy.

Timing is everything

There is a fine balance between hiring on time and hiring late. Timing is everything. If you hire people too soon, you'll find that you aren't ready and your new employees might arrive without equipment or projects. If you hire too late, you might find that your project runs behind and you fail to deliver on time.

It may seem like I'm stating the obvious, but I can't tell you how many times I've arrived at a company on the first day to find that there was no equipment ready or nothing to work on. I inevitably sat around for a few days not doing much. For a startup trying to save money, this is a total waste of resources. With clever planning, you can ensure that, at the very least, the minimum required equipment is ready on day one for your new employee.

Regardless of the roles that you're hiring for, try and get all the timings synchronised. Do you have a project for the employee to work on? If you're hiring a salesperson, have you evaluated your tech startup's selling ecosystem? Does your software engineer have the equipment he or she needs to start building?

To ensure that I have all of my timings worked out, I like to begin by planning from the required start date backward and creating a simple hiring timeline. For example, if you have a position that needs to be filled within two months' time, try and work backward from that.

Task	Days before employee start date
Create Job Description	60-90
Review Job Description	58
Broadcast Job Description	56
Source Candidates	50
Interview Candidates	48
Confirm Candidate	35
Finalise and Send Contract	32
Order Software and Equipment	10
Employee Start Date	0

A sample table showing the tasks to be completed before an employee's start date along with when they should be completed. The colour in each row represents the urgency of each task, moving from green to red, with red being absolute.

As you can see from the timeline above, several steps need to take place before the employee starts day one. The amount of time and the number of steps may differ in each circumstance, but building a simple timeline like this will give you a clear understanding of the tasks that need to be done and by when.

Using a timeline like this allows you to be proactive about planning instead of reacting and struggling to cope with the hiring workload. If you've ever been involved in a large round of hiring, you're aware of how quickly things can spiral out of control when you don't have a plan in place. Try and create one for each role before you embark on your next round of hiring. Set regular calendar reminders to chase the different events in your timeline. It can go a long way toward ensuring that your hiring project stays on track.

When combined with an org chart, a hiring timeline takes you a step further in not only getting a clear idea about **what** you're hiring for, but it also helps you plan for **when** you should be working on hiring. I like to use these two in conjunction to help make the hiring process as smooth as possible.

Calculating the full cost of a new

employee

As you would expect, the budget dictates the scope of your hiring and is often a key limiting factor. When you start the hiring process, it can be easy to underestimate the full costs involved. At first glance, it might seem like the base salary is the only thing you need to keep an eye on, but there's much more involved--costs associated with a new employee that aren't immediately apparent and need to be taken into account include added expenses such as employment taxes, benefits, office equipment, pension fund, software licences, and training costs, to name just a few! Let's say, for example, that we want to hire a new UX Designer with a base salary of 50,000. Ignore the fact that there's no currency involved and that the amount might not match a real salary (this is a hypothetical example).

The table below shows this base salary along with costs such as pension, equipment, training, and insurance.

Expense Name	Cost
Base Salary - per year	50,000
Pension - per year	5,000
Software Licences	1,200
Equipment (Computer, etc.)	1,200
Training - per year	2,000
National Insurance - per year	8,000
Recruitment Fees (@ 20% of base salary)	10,000
Actual cost per year	77,400

As you can see, the expenses associated with an employee quickly add up and cost far more than the initial expected amount. Note that I also included the fees that a recruitment agency is likely to ask for, although this amount isn't a recurring fee but rather will be associated with an employee's first year.

When it comes to hiring employees, I like to think of their actual expense as 1.5 times the base salary. This isn't an exact formula, but a heuristic that you can use to quickly calculate the actual cost of employing a new member of staff.

Although it can be useful to know the full costs, the purpose of this example isn't to scare you off from hiring someone but rather to make you aware of these costs when embarking on a large round of hiring. The last thing you want to do is send out contracts and buy equipment for new employees only to find out that you can't afford them in a few months! That could be a pretty embarrassing experience.

Creating a job description

To get a clear picture of the kinds of roles that you're looking to fill, it's worth starting with the job description. Once you define it, the job description will also give you a clear idea about how to market and "sell" the role. Remember, potential candidates are your customers, and you want to appeal to them.

The job description plays a vital role in the recruiting process; I like to think of it as a product requirements document, or rather, a "people requirements document". It defines what you're looking for and the key responsibilities, and also lets the candidate know what your company is all about. In this section, we'll run through the basic guidelines for creating a great job description as well as some gotchas that you should avoid.

Having job descriptions defined for the roles you're trying to fill goes a step beyond helping you understand **what** you're looking for--it's also key to understanding **how** you're going to hire for these roles. Are you going to use inbound recruiting (e.g. social media, SEO) to hire for this role or a mix of internal and external recruiters? These types of questions are important to understanding the direction you want to take your hiring.

Once you have a clear idea of the role you're looking to fill, creating a job description will clearly define that role. You should tell readers what they're going to do on a daily basis, the projects they might potentially work on, and the kind of hours you expect them to work. By giving the reader enough information, you help them determine whether they want to work for you or not.

There are no hard and fast rules for creating a job description, but it should include a few basic things.

The figure on the below gives you an understanding of the basic format for a job description. You may find that your job descriptions vary slightly in order and length, but the key components are generally the same. To communicate a consistent message, it's worth
solidifying this job description template across your entire company. Each and every role you hire for should follow an agreed upon template.

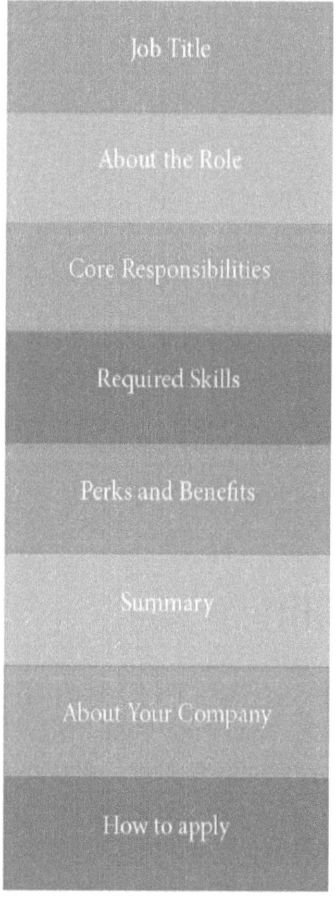

In chapter 2, we talked about how you should hire for cultural fit and how to integrate it into your job descriptions. Ensuring that you have a consistent message across all job descriptions is a great way to do this.

It's important to remember that job descriptions are living documents that constantly need updating and adjusting. As you learn about what does and doesn't work, tweak and update the document to get the best results. Let's look at some of the basic job description sections in closer detail.

Job title

For the job title, keep it simple and start with something specific. For example, if you're looking for a mobile developer who will specialise in iOS development, the title should reflect this: use "iOS Developer" instead of "Mobile Developer".

About the role

As you get into the details about the role itself, start with a small introductory sentence to give the reader an idea about the day-to-day environment. Answering a few questions can help you get started:

- What is the style of the team? Do team members share common interests or have a similar technical background?
- Is there something unique or special about this team?
- How many hours will this role require?
- Will the employee be required to travel?
- What specific challenges does this team face?

Core responsibilities

By giving the reader a compelling story about your company, you distinguish yourself amongst the many others out there. The story should excite people about the possibility of working at your company. Once you've given the reader a basic idea about what the role is about, provide a few bullet points about some of the responsibilities and requirements for the role. Think about specific tasks that might be performed on a day-to-day basis.

Keep the core responsibilities to no more than 6 bullet points--you want to give the reader a concise list that doesn't ramble on. If you can't summarise the core responsibilities in 6 or fewer bullet points, your understanding of the role may be too vague.

From here, lead into some core expectations that you have for this role prior to the candidate joining your company. Again, stick to 6 or fewer bullet points to keep the requirements concise.

Perks and benefits

It's time to finish off the job description with some detail about the job's perks and benefits. Adding benefits such as insurance, pension, and vacation days gives the reader an idea about what to expect when joining your company. This is also your chance to get creative--many startups offer interesting perks, such as weekly breakfasts, dog-friendly offices, free fruit bowls, closing early on summer Fridays, and beer o'clock events.

As we've already discussed in chapter 2, perks shouldn't be confused with culture, but they can help reinforce that there are great benefits to the role other than just working with a great team.

About your company

Your job description might be the first time someone has heard of your company, so it's important to convey a clear message and inspire people to want to learn more about you. Explaining more about your organisation by answering the following questions can steer you in the right direction:

- What does your product/company do?
- What are your core values/culture?
- How big is your company?
- Statistically speaking, how does your company fare in the marketplace?
- How do you stack up compared to your competitors?
- Where do you see the organisation in the next few years?

As you explain your company, keep the details short and clear. The last thing you want to do is bore the reader with information that isn't relevant to the role. After all, most job descriptions are simple adverts.

In chapter 2, we discussed why cultural fit is so important to the success of your business and your hiring strategy. Think about these things when you write about your company. When you find yourself competing against larger organisations with more money and a lot more resources, it can be extremely challenging to compete for great talent, which is why it's so important to focus on your competitive advantages as a company. Take the time to think about what your company does best and exploit that to your advantage as much as possible.

Get it reviewed

Before I consider any job description to be complete, I like to get it reviewed by someone else. This may seem obvious, but it helps iron out any kinks in the details and makes sure that it conveys the right message. I find that it's even better to get the team that the new hire is for to review the job description. Giving the team the opportunity to be involved in the hire from the start helps them feel like they're part of the process and gives them a sense of responsibility.

The truth is that you aren't going to be able to see all the different angles and perspectives of your team and the people who are currently doing the role daily. If everyone participates, the team will help you provide a clear message about the role and the type of person you should be looking for.

Male and female job descriptions

In chapter 2, we ran through why diversity in your office is key to building a great environment and ultimately a great product. To encourage diversity, it's always worth assessing how your job descriptions appear to all genders. Researchers from the Technische Universität München (TUM) showed 260 participants' employment ads for management positions[1]. If the ads used words commonly associated with men, such as "assertive", "independent", "aggressive", and "analytical" interested female candidates said they didn't find the job appealing and were less likely to apply. The last thing you want to do is scare off potential talent by writing gender-biased job descriptions.

This isn't to say that you shouldn't use certain words in your job descriptions, but rather that you should strive to find a balance. It's worth asking friends or colleagues, both male and female, how the job description comes across to them and whether changes are needed.

Salary and package

Many companies like to include the salary in the job description when they broadcast the role to the public. Depending on your organisation, you might even be legally required to show it. Options vary from company to company, but I personally prefer to exclude salary from the job description. Let me explain why.

It might seem as if you aren't being particularly transparent about the role if you don't mention salary, but remember that you only have one chance to attract potential candidates. If the salary doesn't quite match their expectations, they could move on without giving your company another thought. If you're able to be flexible with the salary, adding the amount to the job advert might scare the reader off, and your flexibility might not come across to them. Interested candidates may be deterred if the salary seems too low for them; the inclusion of salary can come across as "closed for negotiation", which isn't always the case.

Another downside is that external organisations have open access to your salary information, meaning you could find yourself in a salary war with a candidate and another organisation, not to mention the fact that your employees could find themselves being headhunted and offered higher salaries from your competitors. As an organisation, disclosing a salary on a job description can also create tension in your organisation. If current employees find this salary information, it can cause unrest when new hires come on, especially if current staff earn less in a similar role.

Once potential candidates have reached out to you and enquired more about the role, this is a perfect opportunity to explain more about the salary and the perks associated with the role. After all, you're looking for candidates who love what they do and aren't simply trawling through job listings looking for a high salary!

The competition

If you're in the process of creating a new job description, you might want to look at your competitors. Focus on the way they structure and present the roles that they're hiring for. Are any perks mentioned that you offer but haven't thought of listing? How do they describe the role?

Normally, "borrowing" ideas is considered a little controversial, but when it comes to job descriptions, the gloves are off! Look at a wide variety of different competitors or organisations in similar industries to yours and use their job descriptions as inspiration for your own. You don't want to create a clone, but rather get inspiration from other sources. After all, you could potentially find yourself competing with these organisations for a candidate. Writing great job descriptions involves being a little sneaky, too!

How do you hire people for a role that you don't understand?

As your startup begins to grow, you might find yourself in a position where you need to hire someone for a role that you don't understand or will never be able to do. This can be a tricky situation, but the reality is that the likelihood of this happening becomes higher as your organisation grows.

My background is developing software for the web, and I feel comfortable enough to hold my own while interviewing someone for a role within that scope, but as soon as you move outside of that, new roles become a bit more difficult for me. I remember a while ago I needed to hire a senior iOS Engineer to be the first member of a new team. While most programming languages share similar concepts, it was scary to know that I was in over my head when it came to this role.

Creating a job description for a role that you aren't familiar with can be challenging in itself. However, a few tactics can make the process a little smoother.

Research the role

Before diving headfirst into defining the role's responsibilities, do a little research first. We've already seen how looking at the competition can give you an edge when hiring for a role. Similarly, you can use the competition to give you an idea of what the market is looking for.

The web can be your best friend when it comes to hiring for a role that you have no experience with. For example, if you're recruiting for a Big Data Engineer, find out some basic principles that revolve around this role. What software should the candidate be familiar with? What are the pros and cons of each? These are generic questions, and you should have a basic idea of a few of them before hiring for the role. While the web won't be able to answer every question, it will help you understand the core principles for the role at hand. Spend some time researching--it will only pay off in the long run.

Rely on others

Much like you would use online recommendations when booking a holiday, you should rely on others to give you feedback about the role definition. Asking for feedback from other people, such as your peers and colleagues, can be a great way to improve your chances of attracting the right talent.

If you have colleagues or people you have worked with before who you can trust, running through a resume or a set of questions with them can give you an edge before an interview. I often find that some of the best advice I get is from my network of friends.

Hire for cultural fit

In chapter 2, we discovered how each new hire that you make can ultimately contribute to building or eroding the culture that you've worked to create. This is why it's so important to hire with a cultural fit in mind.

When you hire people who are a good cultural fit, there's a greater likelihood that they'll easily integrate into the teams and become a contributing member of the company quickly. Having the right skills to do the job is vitally important to the role, but if you ensure that you hire for cultural fit, you will at least have one part of the hiring process tamed.

Relax

You've researched the role, conferred with colleagues about the job description, and aimed for a cultural fit--all you can do now is relax. You've put in the hard work, and you'll always have the opportunity to assess skills when the new hire joins your company.

Select someone who matches your requirements, has the right character and attitude, exhibits the appropriate behaviors, and is qualified to perform the job. After that, all you can do is trust that you've done everything in your power to hire the best person for the role.

If things don't work out a few months down the line, you might find yourself having awkward conversations with the person--in the worst case, you might even have to fire the person. Unfortunately, this is a risk that you have to take and is a very worst-case scenario.

Plan for the busy times

When you approach any new round of hiring, it's inevitable that it will affect your workforce. Planning, preparing, and interviewing all take time, and it's very likely that your projects will suffer as a result.

If you're about to hire one or two people, the impact on your projects might not be that bad, but as you start to hire more and more people, things eventually begin to stack up. As the hiring manager, you want to minimize disruption to your teams and projects as much as possible while at the same time accelerating team growth. It's can be tricky to balance, but with proper planning in place it can be avoided.

The negative impact of a large round of hiring is often unavoidable and can affect your teams and projects. There is a famous saying in the military called the 7 Ps:[2]

"Proper planning and preparation prevents piss poor performance"

While this may seem a little extreme and only applicable to life-or-death situations in the military, this saying highlights the fact that with proper planning, you can avoid poor performance. Taking this into account when planning for a round of hiring goes a long way to help reduce the negative effects associated.

If the opportunity arises, try and spread the hiring load amongst the team. By giving more junior members of your team the ability to participate in the hiring process, you can give them a sense of responsibility and ownership. It's also a great opportunity to help them grow and progress this area of their personal skills. I like to be as transparent about the hiring process as possible, keeping everyone updated on the progress of any new hires. Using something as simple as an organisational chart and keeping it updated is a good way to ensure that everyone is aware of the hiring process and how things are progressing. If it's kept in the forefront of people's minds, it might help reduce disruption when planning for projects.

Summary

- When you approach a round of hiring, no matter how big or small, planning is key to its success.
- A classic organisational chart can be the best way to understand how your teams should be structured.
- Think about the timing involved in placing a hire. It may take longer than you think.
- The cost of a new employee is higher than just the initial base salary. When calculating the overall salary for a new employee, multiplying the base salary by 1.5 is a good guideline of what to expect.
- A well-defined job description will help you understand what types of skills you need to hire for and how you are going to hire for the role.
- Before you put a job description out for the world to see, get it reviewed by someone you trust. It can be helpful to get another person's perspective on the role.
- Don't forget to plan for the busy times. As the saying goes "proper planning prevents piss poor performance"!

References

1. TUM.de - Women do not apply to "male-sounding" job postings - https://www.tum.de/en/about-tum/news/press-releases/short/article/31438
2. Wikipedia.org - 7 Ps (military adage) - https://en.wikipedia.org/wiki/7_Ps_(military_adage)

Chapter 5 - Working with Recruiters

As your startup begins to grow and expand, hiring at scale starts to become tougher, and relying solely on your network and inbound recruiting isn't always the best option. There comes a point in every large round of hiring when you need help. When you're at the early stages of a startup, money is extremely tight, and the idea of spending it on recruitment fees isn't going to be popular. Using the inbound recruiting techniques that we discussed in chapter 3 will go a long way toward helping you build a stream of potential candidates, but when you need to hire at scale, you're going to need as much help as you can get.

Recruitment agents can be a valuable asset if your company can afford them. In this chapter, we'll take a closer look at internal and external recruiters and how you can use both to improve your chances of hiring great talent. We'll start by looking at the recruitment funnel and how each stage plays a part in the wider recruitment picture.

The recruitment funnel

Before we look at the differences and advantages between internal and external recruiters, it's important that we touch on the recruitment funnel. A recruitment funnel is simply a list of candidates that are interested in a particular role and the different stages that they are at in the interview process. When it comes to hiring a new employee, you will go through several stages before you make your final hiring decision. Using a recruitment funnel helps you easily see how many potential hires you may have and at which stage they are at in the hiring process at any given moment. As a hiring manager, it's especially important that you understand how the recruitment funnel works, as it will help you communicate effectively with recruiters and fine-tune the hiring process along the way.

In the same way that a visitor to your website goes through different stages of a funnel, your candidates will enter a recruitment funnel. The recruitment funnel will vary from organisation to organisation and even position to position, but here's the basic idea:

A basic recruitment funnel.

It may seem like a simple concept, but the beauty of using something as simple as this funnel allows you to easily identify how many candidates you currently have in your recruitment funnel and in what stage they are at; the table below is a quick example.

	New	Review	Recruiter Phone Interview	Technical Phone Interview	On-Site Interview	Offer	Hire	Decline
QA Engineer	2	1	0	0	0	0	1	2
Product Manager	5	1	0	2	1	0	0	10

A recruitment funnel helps you see exactly how many candidates are at each stage in the hiring process.

In the table, you can see that we're hiring for two roles. Let's take the first role, QA Engineer, and break down what the pipeline looks like:

- 6 candidates entered the recruitment funnel.
- There are 2 new candidates.
- 1 person is currently being reviewed.
- 1 hire has been made.
- 2 candidates were declined.

We can then take the data from the recruitment funnel and identify the conversion rate for a particular role at each stage of the funnel. This data gives us a good starting point for calculating conversion rates for this role. We can deduce that 1 out of every 6 candidates, or 17%, were successfully hired for this role.

If we take this even further, we can see that 3 candidates made it to the **On-Site Interview** stage (1 hire + 2 decline) with only 1 person successfully being hired, which lets us know that around 33% people who apply for this role are successful. Using this information, we could assume that if we wanted to hire 10 people for this role, we would need to interview 33 people on-site. Once you start to understand your conversion rates, you can work backward to determine what you need to pipe into the top of the funnel to hit your targets.

Using a recruitment funnel is a great way to detect potential issues in your hiring process and find ways to tweak it as you proceed. Let's take another look at the table above, but this time for the second role, Product Manager. We can see a healthy pipeline of new candidates who are interested in this role and that there are a few still in the early stages of the funnel. Most of the numbers look normal, but the **Decline** column shows that 10 candidates were declined which looks slightly higher than the rest of the columns. We can draw many conclusions from this, but it's very possible that the quality of candidates coming in isn't high enough. We could take a number of actions from this, including tightening up the **Phone Interview** stage or even updating the job description to match stricter criteria. The important thing is that you have this data at hand in order to make the right decisions when needed.

Hiring takes time, and refining the process by using something as simple as a recruitment funnel can go a long way toward speeding up your hiring process. The easiest way to make confident decisions is to use the data at your disposal.

Internal and external recruiters

Whether you're a founder, CEO, or hiring manager, it's always best to start by hiring within your own network in the early stages of a startup. The reality is that after a while, your contacts and interested candidates in your network will start to dry up, and you're going to need help hiring. Ellie Romer-Lee, a good friend and Head of Talent at Onfido says:

"If you are going to hire 50 people in the near future, you are going to need help!"

This is where recruiters come in. Over the past few years, there has been a resurgence in the number of organisations creating internal recruitment teams. These teams consist of recruiters who are employed by and work directly for the organisation. There are several advantages to using internal recruiters versus external ones, and if you're lucky enough to work in a company that employs internal recruiters, the benefits are often immediately obvious. Large technology organisations such as Google, Amazon, and Facebook all use internal recruiters because they understand the competitive nature of the market. As we progress through this chapter, we'll explore this role more.

External recruiters, on the other hand, aren't directly employed by the organisation but are contracted to hire for a specific role or roles. You may be familiar with this more traditional approach to hiring--perhaps even contacted by an external recruitment agent in the past. Often known as agencies, headhunters, or search consultants, they act as a middleman and if a candidate is successfully hired, they receive a commission from the organisation. These agencies often specialise in hiring for a certain profession or location and can be a great way to quickly fill a unique role.

The advantages of working with internal recruiters

Regardless of the size of your organisation, building and growing your brand is important. In fact, brand and culture are often the only things that a candidate might come in contact with before spending time at your company. Because internal recruitment teams work with you and are often embedded in your department, they understand the culture and vibe in the office. If you've ever spoken to an internal recruiter on the phone, you often get the sense that they have a good understanding of what the hiring manager is looking for and what the organisation is like (and they should--they work there too!).

Let's take a closer look at the advantages of internal recruiters.

Part of the team

If you're actively involved in recruiting and your organisation employs internal recruiters, working together can go a long way toward helping you hire the best talent out there. Because they're so embedded into your organisation, they're part of the team and understand the culture and vibe in the office. This goes even further when hiring new candidates because if recruiters spend time with the teams, they'll have an understanding about where to place the new candidate.

Some of the best internal recruiters I've worked with are active in the community and constantly tweet and attend conferences. They actually care about the success of the organisation and will aim to hire people that fit the culture and improve overall success.

Lower costs

External recruiters generally charge a commission fee for placing a new employee in an organisation. Internal recruitment teams differ in that they're paid a set salary by the organisation, thus making costs much more predictable. In fact, the British Heart Foundation was able to decrease recruitment spending by just over 50% after it created an in-house recruitment team[1].

Over time, internal recruiters become more than just a money saver. Startups in the early stages can be chaotic, busy, and wonderful places to work at--there's so much to do and limited resources available to get things done. The idea of spending time and money on hiring often seems painful, but by hiring an internal recruiter (or recruitment team), you save not only money in the long run but also time. Internal recruiters are constantly searching for new candidates, filtering CVs, and interviewing potential candidates--tasks that you don't have to take on.

While there may be peaks and troughs in your hiring, the day job for internal recruitment agents doesn't stop, and you'll often find them on social media spreading the word about your organisation. As we've discussed in earlier chapters of this book, the concept of building brand awareness around your company and promoting hiring should be a continuous one.

When you should hire internal recruiters

Are you planning on hiring regularly over the next year? Or will the hiring be sporadic and less frequent?

If you're able to answer these two questions, you can decide whether it's worthwhile hiring internal recruiters. If you only intend to hire a few people over the next few years, the paid salary of an internal recruiter might exceed the costs that you would otherwise pay an external recruiter. However, if you intend to hire at scale, your best option is definitely internal recruiters. That said, if you're in the early stages of a startup and not necessarily well funded, it might be best to try and hire yourself or use an external recruiter for specialist roles at short notice. External recruiters are great when it comes to hiring for specific roles and locations.

In larger organisations, I've seen internal recruiters use the services of external recruiters to place a role within their organisation. While this may work well for very specific, one-off roles, it can become costly to employ an internal recruiter and then use the skills of an external recruiter at the same time. While it does improve your chances of hiring, you might find that your internal recruiters are just acting as the middleman and managing external agencies. This costs you twice as much money and can mean you're paying a salary for someone who acts as an administrator. Note: If you already have an established HR department, some of these administrative duties might fall to them, leaving the internal recruiter with little to work on.

Hiring an internal recruiter or recruitment team can be very beneficial to your organisation and has many merits, but without proper planning it can actually cost you money in the long run. If you can't honestly say whether you'll be hiring consistently over a given time period, it might be best to look toward external recruiters.

How to work effectively with internal recruiters

The most important part of working effectively with internal recruiters is to actually care about the hiring process. While this may seem a little harsh, I often come across managers who hate hiring and are too busy to work closely with an internal recruiter to fill a role. They're often slow in responding and difficult to get hold of, which forces the internal recruiter to constantly chase them.

The truth is that internal recruiters are on your side and actually want to fill that open role just as much as you do. By working closely with them, you'll get the most out of the hiring experience and their expertise at the same time. After many rounds of hiring and speaking to many recruiters, there are a few things that I always like to keep in mind. Let's have a look at a few tips that will help you work effectively when dealing with recruiters.

Stay in contact

Whether you're recruiting for one or several roles, organise regular catch ups to keep up to date at every stage of the process. During hiring rounds, it's often helpful to arrange regular, short meetings with all the stakeholders involved in the process. Using something as simple as the org chart that we discussed in chapter 4 can be a great way to look at the open roles you may be hiring for. Another useful tool is the recruitment funnel as it can quickly give current hiring process status.

Don't wait to be pestered. Even during busy periods, it pays to quickly check in with the recruiter and find out about open roles. Working together effectively involves communication and a common understanding of what you're trying to achieve. For a hiring manager, internal recruiters are happy to help, and checking in occasionally can only help improve the entire process for both of you.

Be patient

As we've discovered in earlier chapters of this book, finding the next great member of your team takes time. Once you've created an open role and the job description is live, relax and rely on the internal recruiter to fill the role. Don't expect to see a list of candidates on your desk an hour after you've sent out a job description.

Plan ahead

During busy times, trying to fit in a round of hiring can be stressful and feel like low priority. This is where internal recruiters can be your best ally. By planning ahead and giving them your availability, they can easily shuffle and organise the hiring around your schedule. The best internal recruiters are capable of making the hiring process a lot smoother for you.

Because internal recruiters work for the same organisation as you, they're able to book meeting rooms and can often send meeting invites accordingly. For a busy manager, this can make your life much easier.

Be realistic

If you're an early-stage startup and have just acquired your first round of funding, it can be tempting to think of yourself as the next Slack or Docker, two very successful startups. While this may one day come true, the reality is that many people haven't yet heard of your organisation. The competition is fierce out there, and smart talent isn't going to work for you just because your company is growing quickly. By being realistic about your organisation and with the recruiter, you have the best chance of success.

Get back to them

After you've finished interviewing a candidate, giving feedback as soon as possible to the internal recruiter is a great way to ensure that you get quick turnaround on the role. As busy as things may be, hiring should be a top priority and getting back to the recruiter can speed up the whole process significantly. Regardless of whether the candidate was successful in the interview, a quick response time lets the recruiter understand whether to continue the process.

As with any great team, communication and teamwork are key to success. Even though it may be for short bursts of time, I like to think of the internal recruiter as part of my team. Things will work much more effectively if we are in sync.

How to work effectively with external recruiters

Depending on the size and maturity of your organisation, employing an internal recruiter might not be the best option right now. However, the ability to hire an external recruitment agency can be a good way to help fill an open role in the short term. Many recruitment agencies have specialist recruiters that will search for candidates by a particular location or skill. If you aren't hiring on a regular basis, external recruiters can be a great way to find the talent that you need.

In the same way that internal recruiters can make the hiring process a lot smoother, external recruiters can also be a great asset when it comes to hiring great talent.

Arrange a visit

While this may seem like an obvious one, very few organisations take the time to show external recruiters around the office. Remember that they don't have a feel for what it's like to work for you or what your office even looks like. Arrange a visit and take the time to show them around. It will help you engage with the recruiter and set a welcoming tone from the start of the working relationship.

Stay in contact

In the same way that it's important to stay in contact with internal recruiters, it's just as important to keep communicating with external recruitment agencies. It may not always be possible to arrange face-to-face meetings, but regular, short catch ups on the phone/Skype can be a great way to keep all stakeholders up to date on the progress of any hires. Using tools such as the org chart and recruitment funnel can be a great way to assess the state of your hiring progress.

Michelle Flynn, an experienced recruiter and a good friend, says, *"Treat the recruitment agency in the same way you would a business supplier or business partner"*. She goes on to say, *"Give them feedback and regular information, and you'll find that an agency partnership can work really well"*.

You get what you pay for

As with most things in life, you tend to get what you pay for. Most recruitment agencies have a set fee that they charge for placing each new hire. As an early stage startup, it can be tempting to try and knock this fee down as low as possible. But although you may only be able to afford a lower fee, it's worth remembering that most agencies work with multiple companies, so they'll prioritise the roles that give them a higher placement fee, which means you might be a third or fourth choice for a great candidate.

On the flip side, it's worth mentioning that recruitment agencies do take on a lot of risk. You only pay them when they successfully place someone with you, and they have to pay for any advertising costs to get the role across to as many people as possible.

Keep the numbers down

If you're urgently looking to fill a position, it can be very tempting to try and spread the hiring and work with as many agencies as possible. After all, you only pay when they place a candidate with you, right? Well, this is partly true, but in the long run, it can actually slow down the hiring process.

As a general rule, most agencies won't want to send over the resume for a candidate who might have already been sent to you by another agency. As you start to spread the net and use more agencies, there's a greater chance of this happening. The same candidate may have passed through quite a few agencies, which might end up slowing the process down.

As a personal preference, I prefer to stick to one agency to start with, and if it can't find suitable candidates within a predetermined timeframe, it's time to move on. By sticking to just one or two agencies at a time, you also lower the administration costs. It can be very time-consuming, constantly bouncing between agencies and arranging catch up meetings. As a hiring manager, your time is precious, and the last thing you want to do is spend all your time dealing with external agencies.

Beware the sting

Working with external recruiters can be a great way to find talent and help save time when it comes to hiring. As I've mentioned, if you treat the agency as a business partnership, the relationship can work well. However, recruitment is a cut throat business that has a bad reputation among many businesses. While this sounds like a sweeping statement, most recruitment agencies won't have your best interests at heart and often look to place the candidate without any further thought about the success of your organisation.

Put another way, recruitment agencies want to fill the role as much as you do, but their allegiances don't always lie in the same place. They have goals and sales targets that need to be met, with monthly salaries on the line. The competition for great talent is fierce, and I've seen recruiters employ some rather unscrupulous methods for hiring, including trying to poach a star employee behind my back.

The unfortunate truth is that many of your employees are constantly bombarded with emails and calls by recruitment agencies looking to place them somewhere else. It's a dog-eat-dog world out there, and recruiters are trying everything they can to place candidates. It's important to lay the ground rules from the start when dealing with agencies. If you find that an agency is trying to poach members of your staff to work elsewhere whilst helping place staff with you at the same time, it's absolutely time to move on.

When you find an agency that you can trust, and the relationship works effectively, stick with it. While many agencies do use shady tactics to hire candidates, not all agencies are created equal. It's easy to paint all recruiters with the same brush, but it's important to understand the challenges that you face and avoid the sting you may face without that knowledge in place.

Summary

*   The recruitment funnel can help you easily understand how many potential hires you may have and at which stage they are in the overall process.
*   When you need to hire at scale, it becomes a lot tougher managing the recruitment pipeline as well as your day-to-day role; internal and external recruiters can be a great asset to your company when searching for talent on a bigger scale.
*   An internal recruitment team is embedded into the organisation and understands the culture and vibe in the office.
*   If you plan on hiring at irregular intervals, recruitment agencies can be a better option than internal recruiters.
*   Be careful when dealing with external recruitment agencies: they want to fill the role as much as you do, but they won't always have your best interests at heart. If you find an agency and have a good working relationship, stick close to them, as it can be very fruitful in the long run.

References

1. Recruiter.co.uk - The Rise of the Internal Recruiter - http://www.recruiter.co.uk/archive/part-28/The-rise-of-the-internal-recruiter

Chapter 6 - The Interview Process

As we've progressed through this book, our main focus has been on attracting talent and planning for hiring. Now comes the big part: it's time to meet with the candidate. This is a crucial stage in the whole hiring process because it's a chance for you and your team to find out more about the person and assess whether he or she is the right fit for your organisation. In this chapter, we'll learn about the importance of interview training for everyone involved, as well as sound advice for the phone and on-site interviews. By the end of the chapter, you should have a solid idea of how interviews are run by some of the most well-known startups around the world.

The different stages of the interview process

If you think about it for a second, the traditional interview process seems a bit crazy. You meet with someone for an hour or so, ask her a few questions about her background, and if she seems up to the job, you trust her to join your organisation and invest loads of time and effort. Crazy, right? In this chapter, I'm going to challenge the traditional interview process and break down each stage so that you can get the most out of the candidate and find out if he or she is really the right fit for your team.

Different startups have different approaches to interviews. It's about finding which method works best for you. You may be an early-stage startup that hasn't figured out a standard format for your interview process and plays each interview by ear, or maybe you already have something more formal in place but aren't quite sure about the best approach yet. Regardless of the maturity of your organisation, it's important to find out what works best for you and stick to it as a standard format. In the really early stages of a startup, it's easy to be disorganised when it comes to the interview. This might be acceptable in the short run, but you'll quickly learn that a laissez-faire approach won't scale going forward.

By using a set of distinct phases during the interview, you'll create a template for going forward that will help you plan for each interview, train new interviewers on the hiring process, and scale the process as the organisation grows. Here's one example:

A standard interview process can be broken down into different stages.

While this table may seem simple and obvious, having a standard interview process in place will serve as the basis for all the roles you need to hire for to fill in your organisation. By standardising your interview process, you'll get consistent results and also find it easier to train new managers on the interview process.

Remember; good interviews take time

In many organisations around the world, it isn't uncommon for on-site interviews to only last an hour or even 30 minutes. For a lot of companies, this is considered a standard length and is often adopted as de facto. The reality is that good interviews take time, and the more time you spend with the candidate, the more you'll get out of the hiring process. The problem with interviews that only last for an hour is that it's hard to evaluate someone that quickly. This is even truer when you're hiring for more technical roles: you really should spend some time and get inside the brain of the person you're interviewing.

Instead of a typical one-hour on-site interview, extend it to, say, two or three hours and rotate the interviewers. As we've already discussed, having two different people at each stage of the process gives you a well-rounded view of the candidate. But instead of asking the same questions with different interviewers over three hours, split the interview into stages. For example, an on-site interview for a software engineer might look a little something like this:

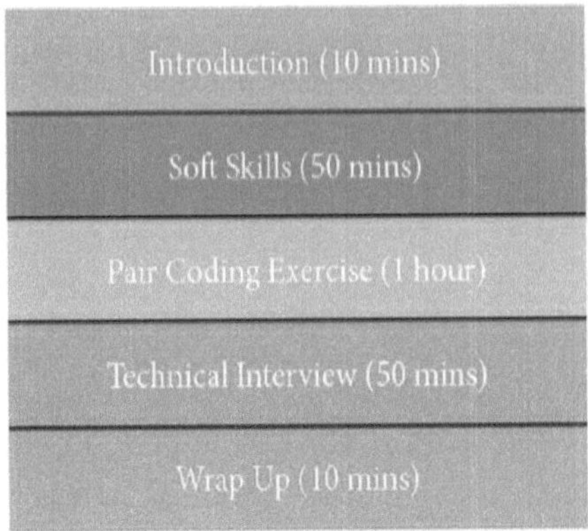

The interview stages are broken down into smaller chunks of time that give you a holistic view of the candidate's skills. Over the three hours, you'll get a glimpse into their soft skills (teamwork, cultural fit, interpersonal skills, and communication) as well as their technical skills.

As an added bonus, the coding exercise let's them see the job's day-to-day responsibilities. As a potential candidate, I would be pretty impressed if I got the chance to spend more time with the team of people I might be working with than just a rushed, one-hour interview. Yes, it takes time to go through several candidates and spend a few hours each, but I can almost guarantee that it will cut down on the number of bad hires you will make. After a number of your trusted interviewers have spent time with the candidate, and the vote is a resounding "yes!", you'll know you're onto a winner.

Before the interview

Some interviewers are complete naturals. They have this ability to make the candidate and everyone in the room feel at ease and get the best out of the person they're interviewing. But such people are usually made not born--rare is the person who has this ability from his or her first interview. I remember when I started interviewing candidates how nervous and filled with anticipation I was at the thought of it. What if the candidate realises that this is my first interview? What if he asks me a question about the company that I don't know the answer to? All these thoughts and more ran through my head at once.

The reality is that many first-time managers and employees are relatively inexperienced when it comes to interviewing others. When new candidates walk into your offices, you and your employees might be the first face-to-face contact they have with your organisation, which is why first impressions matter so much. Regardless of whether you ultimately end up hiring the candidate, he or she should still enjoy the interview process with you.

But without proper training and understanding of that process, it's easy for first-time managers and employees to make mistakes and give off an air of unprofessionalism. If your startup is relatively new, you need to use every opportunity to turn people into ambassadors for your brand, even if you don't end up hiring them!

Interview training

During my career, I've had the unpleasant experience of being involved in some terrible interviews. In a few minutes, an interview can go from good to downright awkward. If an inexperienced hiring manager fires off a sensitive or shocking question, it only underlines the awkwardness, not to mention the fact that the candidate will almost definitely leave the interview feeling unhappy about the company and the process as a whole.

The unfortunate reality is that many hiring managers and interviewers have never received formal interview training. Without that training in place, it's easy for your interviewers to ask questions that might offend candidates or in some cases even be illegal! This training doesn't have to be time-consuming or in-depth, but at a very minimum, it should cover the following:

- What are the basic stages of the process?
- What types of questions are unacceptable to ask?
- What violates a candidate's rights and privacy?
- How can you identify and hire candidates more objectively?
- How do you hire for cultural fit?

It's worth spending some time teaching first-time interviewers about some of the basic legal rules of interviewing. It might seem unnecessary, but you or one of your interviewers might unintentionally end up discriminating against someone, potentially creating all sorts of problems down the road. Having these rules in place helps prevent discrimination during an interview and protects the candidate involved.

Here are just a few of the questions that you shouldn't ask:

- What is your date of birth? How old are you?
- Do you have any criminal convictions?
- Do you belong to a trade union?
- Are you pregnant?

While some of these questions might seem obvious not to ask, other more subtle questions can easily offend someone. It's important that you train your interviewers on the subject. I'd also recommend checking the legal rules for your country as they will differ depending on your location. The last thing you want to do is spend time creating an awesome candidate experience only to offend someone by not training your interviewers properly!

Another great training technique is to get your first-timers to shadow a more experienced interviewer. They don't need to say much or even question the candidate, but it gives them a good opportunity to watch and learn as much as possible. An experienced interviewer can make everyone in the room feel at ease as well as present an air of confidence that only comes with practice. By watching and learning, your more inexperienced interviewers will quickly learn the ropes. Once your first-timers have a few interviews under the belts, take the time to give them feedback. What should they continue or stop doing? It will help them grow, conduct interviews on their own, and train other first-time hiring managers on the process. As your organisation begins to grow, it won't always be possible for you to attend each and every interview. By training other managers on the process, you'll ensure that hiring scales as your organisation grows. You need to know that you can rely on the people around you to hire great people.

While it may seem like a big-time investment up front, training your employees will equip them to conduct interviews in a professional manner and ensure that they get the most out of the candidate. Due to human nature, mistakes will be made and certain things will be said incorrectly, but with proper training, you can ensure that this is less likely to happen.

Set up a kickoff meeting

Before embarking on interviews, it's worth arranging a kickoff meeting to get all the stakeholders involved right from the start. This meeting serves several purposes, giving you the opportunity to:

- Determine who will be involved at each stage of the interview
- Give stakeholders an idea about which team/department this role belongs to
- Educate everyone about the key skills required for the role
- Ensure that the questions asked are geared toward the role

This meeting doesn't have to be lengthy, but it should get all stakeholders on the same page. If you've ever been an interviewee who received mixed messages during various stages of the process, you know how frustrating it can be. Nothing smacks more of a chaotic startup than a group of interviewers who seemingly haven't talked or discussed what's going on.

It's important for the kickoff meeting to take place before any interviews begin. By establishing a clear plan for each stage, you'll find that you and your team become more efficient and waste less time during the interview process. You'll also find that potential candidates enjoy a much better overall experience--after all, the process is both a buying and a selling one.

Create a list of questions

If you find that you regularly hire for similar roles, create a list of standard questions that you can circulate among everyone involved. For example, if you regularly hire software developers, creating a list of common software interview questions is a great way to ensure that you're consistent in your hiring for that role. I also find that it's a good way to benchmark candidates against one another. Try to build a list of questions for every role to ensure that you're always ready to interview. Resist reading the questions like a script--it's better to weave them into the interview and keep the discussion flowing smoothly. You should still feel the need to go off-page with your questions! The more questions you have, the easier it is to cycle through different ones in an interview.

There are few downsides to creating a list, but I have to mention a big one: employees could circulate them outside of the organisation and give an unfair advantage to potential candidates. I've had the unfortunate experience of working with an external recruiter who somehow got hold of the questions and circulated them to all the candidates they sent for on-site interviews! While there's a risk associated with making a list, mixing up the questions and only using them as a guideline will help guarantee a consistent interview process for candidates and interviewers. It's good to throw in a curveball question every now and then--just make sure it isn't offensive!

Get everyone involved

To get a well-rounded view of any candidate, it's best to have a few people involved instead of just one or two. I find that this serves two purposes: it helps you truly understand the candidate's strengths and weaknesses (each person will interview from a different angle), and if the people involved in the interviews are on the team that this role will ultimately join, it empowers and helps them feel as if they collectively chose the best person. The new candidate is almost immediately accepted by the team as a result.

Unfortunately, there's a tendency among some companies to only use a "chosen few" when it comes to interviews. I like the way that Joel Spolsky, CEO of the Stack Exchange Network, puts it[1]:

"You should always try to have at least six people interview each candidate that gets hired, including at least five who would be peers of that candidate. You know the kind of company that just has some salty old manager interview each candidate, and that decision is the only one that matters? These companies don't have very good people working there."

Relying on a "chosen few" for your interviews might result in a few lucky candidates getting through without a thorough assessment of their skills. It could be hard to include six people in each interview if your company is fairly small, but try to get a well-rounded number of interviewers involved. Regardless of the number of stages in your interview process, having at least two people at every stage is a great baseline.

Get prepared

Before heading into any interview that involves interaction with the candidate, spend some time preparing. Read through the resume, investigate the organisations the person worked for in the past, and prepare a few questions that are specific to the candidate's career history. With preparation, you can dig a little deeper and find areas that might need improvement.

During my pre-interview preparation, I pick out a few key areas of the person's background and mention it during the interview. For example, I might say, "I've had a look at your online portfolio, and I really liked your last project. Tell me more about it." By asking questions specific to the candidate's background, you can lead into questions that pertain specifically to the role that you're hiring for. The candidate can also talk freely about his or her background and use examples to showcase related skills.

Some of the best interviewers I've had the chance to work with allow the interview to flow smoothly by leading into questions as part of a natural conversation. With a little bit of preparation, you'll be surprised how smoothly your interviews start to flow.

It's worth mentioning that preparation also involves planning your time effectively. Check that your schedule is free and that you can devote your full attention to the interview. There's nothing worse than arriving for an on-site interview only to find your interviewers haven't bothered to show up on time or prepare for you. Candidates are very perceptive to the whole interview experience and will easily pick up on the signals that you give off.

To test or not to test?

For many technical roles, it isn't uncommon for organisations to ask candidates to complete a technical test. This can be a great way to determine whether the candidate actually has the day-to-day skills needed to perform the job at hand. I've interviewed many candidates who were really passionate about their career, presented well, got along excellently with the team, and generally seemed like a perfect fit--that is, until it came to the technical test.

If you know that the role will require day-to-day technical work and expertise, it's always advisable to ask the candidate to complete a technical test. Unless you're willing to train for the role, you don't want to find out a month after they join that the person isn't skilled enough to do the work required. When it comes to the technical test, try and make it tough but fun. After all, good candidates want to know that they're being employed by smart people.

It can be quite disheartening when someone who seems perfect for the role stumbles at the technical test. There could be several reasons--nervousness, lack of knowledge, or even misunderstanding the question--but if someone simply can't complete the test successfully, it's highly likely that he or she won't be right for the role. It's not the end of the world, it just means that the candidate might not be right for the role right now with your organisation.

You'll also need to decide where and when this technical test will take place. For example, many companies let candidates do the test from home in their own time, while others prefer the test to take place on site. Personally, I find that getting the candidate on site and using a technique known as "pair programming" works best. Originally intended for agile software development, this technique can be applied to any technical role, and it's a good way to actively observe someone performing a daily task. Pair programming[2] (sometimes referred to as peer programming) is an agile software development technique in which two people work as a pair together at one computer. One person "drives" and works on a technical task, while the "observer" reviews the task and gives feedback along the way. The best way to pair program is to sit side by side in front of the monitor. Start with a boilerplate example and allow the candidate to solve a technical problem that the role may encounter on a daily basis. It's okay to "nudge" the candidate in the right direction if he or she gets stuck, but ultimately you want them to solve the problem. The idea behind the pair programming technique is that it lets you observe how the candidate thinks, while at the same time seeing how he or she collaborates and communicates with others.

Once several candidates complete the technical test, stop and assess how well your tests are going as a whole. Is only a tiny percentage of candidates making it through this stage, or is almost every single candidate passing the test with flying colours? It's a fine balance to strike, because you want the technical test to be challenging but also fun. You might want to adjust accordingly.

How you decide to test for your more technical roles is up to you, but the most important part is that you actually test your candidates. In the long run, you'll save yourself precious time and money by ensuring that each person is able to perform the day-to-day tasks required for the role.

Preparing for the interview: Application review

It can be pretty tough to find out everything that you need to know about someone from a resume, but knowing a few tell-tale things to look out for will help ensure that you don't waste your efforts.

At the very top of the list of things to watch for is passion. Does the candidate's resume reflect a passion for his or her career? It can be quite easy to spot this just by looking out for any side projects or extracurricular activities. If you want to hire a software engineer, does the person have any online examples of work? Does he or she contribute to any open source projects? Do they write a blog? If you're looking to hire a UX designer, does this person have a portfolio of online work or side projects? Are they involved in any design meetups? Having a side project isn't a must, but it's a great indicator that someone enjoys what he or she does enough to do it outside normal working hours. After all, people who are eager to learn and grow their skills are the kind of people you want working for you.

When talking about interviews and candidates, Google's Eric Schmidt says[3]:

"Our ideal candidates are the ones who prefer rollercoasters, the ones who keep learning. These 'learning animals' have the smarts to handle massive change and the character to love it."

In the early stages of a startup, you'll face constant change. Hiring employees who embrace learning are key to growth and success.

Another aspect of a resume that makes it instantly stand out is a cover letter. They might seem rather traditional, but a well-written cover letter indicates that the candidate has taken the time to find out about the role and explain why he or she is worth employing. Many of the resumes that pass through my inbox these days don't have a cover letter attached, but with a little bit of thought and care, such letters make an average resume stand out immediately. Keep an eye out for generic copy-and-paste cover letters; they're the ones that simply have the addressee field updated and could relate to any organisation in the world. They aren't worth the paper they're written on.

When scanning through the resume, what does the candidate's work history look like? Lots of short hops between companies could potentially be a bad sign, so it's worth asking the candidate why he or she moved around. You don't want to take a candidate through the entire interview process, hire them, and then watch them leave you in a few months time for unknown reasons. The hiring process is time-consuming for everyone involved, so avoid serial leavers if possible!

On the other side of the coin, a good sign on a resume is promotion within a company. If someone has been with an organisation for a few years and was promoted during that time, it can be an indicator that someone else thought that this person was worth advancing to the next level. Candidates like these are definitely worth interviewing.

Another thing to look out for on someone's resume is spelling mistakes. Some managers are extremely strict when it comes to typos, but I prefer to be a bit lenient. Sometimes the candidates you interview may be from another country, and your language might not necessarily be their first one. You could potentially miss out on a brilliant employee because of a simple mistake or misunderstanding. Don't get me wrong, if the candidate's resume is littered with mistakes, this should be an automatic "no", but let common sense prevail.

Reviewing resumes isn't easy, and it's never foolproof. There will be times when someone who looked brilliant on paper turned out to be completely wrong for the role, or vice versa. After filtering and reviewing resumes, the next step is to screen the remaining candidates over the phone.

The phone interview

The phone interview is a great opportunity to interact with candidates and find out more about their skills. This stage is normally done by one person and can take anywhere from 30 minutes to an hour. While many organisations don't always include a phone interview stage, I find that it can be a great way to highlight candidates who aren't appropriate. It might seem like an extra step, but you'll be surprised at how many candidates get turned down at this stage. It's a great way to save you and your team time: if you find the candidate isn't quite right at this stage, you will have spent an hour of one person's time instead of six people's time.

When you're on the phone with candidates, determine whether they can communicate effectively. Can they easily articulate what they're trying to say? If they can't, they'll struggle in a team environment.

If the role will require technical expertise, consider diving into a few technical questions over the phone. By running the candidate through a few basic questions, you should get a general feel for the person's level of expertise. After all, the phone interview stage shouldn't be too intense. Use it to find out a bit more about the candidate's background, communication skills, and ability to hold his or her own on the more technical questions. Many organisations that recruit software developers like to test candidates during the phone interview by using online sharing tools such as Google Docs or Microsoft OneDrive. Using these tools and running through a simple coding example can be a useful way to validate whether the candidate is able to perform basic programming tasks. While you might prefer to test the candidate on site instead of using online tools, it can be a great opportunity to test whether he or she is worth bringing in. Running through an example in an hour of one person's time is better than an entire team finding out that the candidate isn't quite right for the role in real time.

By the end of the hiring process, a lot of time will be invested by people throughout your organisation, so any techniques that you can use to reduce this impact while ensuring that you hire the best people available are worth considering.

The on-site interview

Without a doubt, the on-site interview is the most important part of the whole process. It's often the first time that you will meet the candidate face to face, and it's your chance to proudly showcase what your company and the role is all about. I've picked up a few tricks over the years that help ensure that on-site interviews run as smoothly as possible.

Take notes

When you're meeting face to face with a candidate, a lot of things are going on. Unless you have a photographic memory, it can be hard to remember everything that happened in an interview if you were asked about it the next day. This is why it's so important to take notes. For some interviewers, taking notes might seem a bit painful at first, but once you get into the habit, it quickly becomes apparent why it's so useful.

Once the candidate walks out of your office doors, it isn't easy to remember every reason that helped you form an opinion of them. Good notes don't need to record every question and answer, but they should be concise and allow you to easily focus on the candidate during the interview while you jot things down, a few highlights and important areas to follow up on later. Good notes aren't judgemental; they're professional. Don't write anything nasty about the candidate down--he or she could easily sneak a peek! It's also worth remembering that you might need to refer back to your notes in a few days or even weeks, so try and make them as legible as possible. Other interviewers should also take notes, as they might serve to give a wider opinion on a candidate.

In some countries, it's a legal requirement to keep records/notes for a certain period of time. If candidates feel that the interview was unfair or felt discriminated against, they're often within their rights to determine why they weren't hired, and you'll need some record to prove why you thought they weren't right for the role. This is extremely rare, but having good notes is the perfect way to show that you asked professional and unbiased questions.

Prepare the room

A few days before you know that a candidate will be attending an interview with you, ensure that you have a meeting room booked and reserved. In most offices, these rooms are a precious commodity.

On the day of the interview, stop in and make sure the room is clean and tidy before the candidate is due. If the candidate is going to be with you for a few hours, get some water ready and on the table before arrival. With a little bit of preparation, you'll ensure that the candidate feels welcome from the first moment.

I've been in situations where staff constantly knock on the door of a meeting room and interrupt an interview in progress to check if the room is free. This can be a frustrating experience for the candidate and is extremely distracting. If you anticipate that this might happen, place a simple sign and mark the door with "interview in progress" to deter any interruptions. Remember that candidates are your "customers", and that on-site interviews need to be treated with respect!

Coffee shops

If you're in the early stages of a startup, you might share a co-working space with other businesses or even work in a small office without a meeting room. For small startups, a meeting room is a precious commodity that they can ill afford.

Most startups without large facilities look to other sources such as coffee shops, nearby offices, or hired meeting rooms. Whatever option you decide to use, remember that it should be quiet and distraction free. You want to focus on the candidate, and distractions will affect both you and the candidate. I've had the unpleasant experience of interviewing in a noisy coffee shop only to find that by the end of the conversation, we were both raising our voices to be heard!

A good option is to rent a room for the day. If you type *"hire a meeting room"* into Google, you'll be presented with several options in any city around the world. Spending a little extra money on a meeting room will make such a difference to the overall feeling that both you and the candidate will retain after the interview.

Introduction

First impressions count, and you want the candidate to enjoy the hiring experience with your organisation right from the start. I've been on many interviews where I've been left waiting for up to 30 minutes because the hiring manager was running late. While this is sometimes unavoidable and incidents do happen, making it a regular occurrence sends all the wrong signals to potential candidates. When the candidate arrives at your office for the first time, it's important that someone is there to greet him or her immediately.

Interviewing is a nerve-wracking experience for many people, but as hiring managers, we have the ability to calm those nerves and help relax the candidate. I find that a great technique to break the ice is to show the person around the office. Regardless of the size of your organisation, this can be a great way for the candidate to get a feel for the office environment and temporarily take his or her mind off the interviewing at hand. After all, if you were buying a car, you would expect to see what the car looks like before making the purchase. In the same way, the candidate is going to spend every day working in your offices, you should at least show off what it looks like!

Once you give a basic walkthrough of the office, get the candidate settled in the meeting room. Depending on which stage of the interview you have lined up next, everyone involved should be ready to go. At this point, it's worth explaining to the candidate the outline for the interview and how each stage will unfold. Introduce each person involved in the interview and their role in the organisation.

Before diving straight into serious technical or background questions, I like to ask candidates a bit about themselves. Ask them to introduce themselves and tell you what they're interested in and most excited about. I find that this helps the candidate relax and sets the stage for conversation throughout the rest of the interview.

Soft skills

Regardless of the size of your organisation, people who work well together, are friendly, and have good communication skills are key to the harmony of your organisation. These "soft skills" are also referred to as emotional intelligence and are an important part of the hiring equation. As a manager, soft skills are those "fluffier" attributes that are hard to define. Employees who possess these attributes are generally nice people to work with. I like to think that soft skills fall under the umbrella of creativity, listening skills, and team skills.

When interviewing candidates, determining their ability to perform day-to-day work and handle technical problems is essential. However, a key part to any role should be soft skills. After all, you want to hire people who work together harmoniously and are capable of communicating effectively with others. Even if you have the next Bill Gates sitting in front of you, there's no point in making the hire if the person doesn't possess the soft skill attributes required. Some of the questions you might ask at this stage include the following:

- Why are you looking to join this company?
- Tell me about your biggest work failure. What did you learn?
- How would your colleagues describe you? What strengths or weaknesses do you think they would mention?
- Do you have any personal projects? Tell me about them.
- What frustrates you at work?
- Tell me about a time when you had a difficult working relationship with someone. How did you handle it?

Questions like these are designed to test a candidate's learning agility, work ethic, self-awareness, and ability to solve problems. By asking a few simple questions like the ones above, you should be able to build an idea of whether the candidate would work well with the people in your organisation. Many times I've interviewed someone who seemed brilliant technically, only for him or her to respond with a few shocking answers to soft skills questions. This unfortunately resulted in a no hire, but finding this out during the soft skills stage saved many awkward future conversations.

In chapter 2, we talked about the importance of cultural fit in an organisation. The soft skills stage of the interview process is your chance to find out if the candidate is a good cultural fit. Here are some questions that will help assess cultural fit in an interview:

- What type of culture do you thrive in?
- What values are you drawn to, and what's your ideal workplace?
- Tell me about a time when you worked with/for an organisation where you felt you were not a strong cultural fit. Why was it a bad fit?

Remember how we discussed in chapter 2 that a culture should be entwined with your organisation's core values? These core values are the guiding principles or codes of conduct upon which your company was founded and operates under on a daily basis. Depending on the culture of your organisation, you'll want to fashion interview questions around this. For example, if you're a company that lives and breathes sports, you should find out if this candidate is even vaguely interested in sports. It's worth asking yourself if you're looking for people who are passionate about what your organisation does or simply looking for someone to fill the role!

While you can do your best to identify a candidate's soft skills, there will be times when someone is so charming that he or she can answer all the questions with everything that you want to hear. Ask genuine questions and truly assess their soft skills. If a candidate gives you a generic answer that you might find out of a book on a shelf, press for more information. When you begin to dig a little deeper, you'll truly find out if the candidate is right for the role. If they worked on a project, find out exactly what role they played on the project. Were they actually involved from start to finish? Or did they merely help out toward the end?

Earlier in this chapter we talked about creating a list of questions that you can reuse in different interviews. Soft skills questions are a great example of this because every person's answer will be different. Candidates can't memorize a generic answer to soft skills questions because they're based on their own experience and no one else's!

Technical skills

Up until this stage of the on-site interview, you've assessed the soft skills of the candidate and asked questions about cultural fit, but now comes the important part: Does this person have the technical skills to perform the job on a daily basis?

Once the candidate has completed the pair programming exercise, explore his or her work history and technical skills further. Instead of asking a series of quick-fire technical questions, I prefer to get the whiteboard out and ask the candidate to explain his or her most recent role. If the role was as a sales manager, ask the person to draw on the whiteboard and explain the sales process. What did the candidate like or not like about the process? What would she change to improve it? Another example of a technical test might be for a software engineer. Ask the candidate to draw the architecture of his past company on the whiteboard. What did he like about the architecture? What would he change? Using the whiteboard lets you and the candidate visualize past projects and gives you the chance as an interviewer to fashion questions around it.

As you progress through the technical interview, find out the candidate's involvement on each project. Ask questions that help you determine what he or she actually worked on during each project versus what the rest of the team did.

By the end of the technical interview, you should have a clear understanding as to whether the candidate has the skills necessary to perform the job on a daily basis. Your testing and questioning should be challenging but easy enough for a candidate to complete without spending too much time. By testing candidates, you'll find that if they're successful in the interview, it's highly likely that they can hit the ground running and become a contributing member of the team from day one.

Wrap up

Once the interview draws to a close, ensure that you have time to wrap things up. This gives you the perfect opportunity to answer any questions that the candidate might have, as well as explain why yours is such a great company to work for.

In chapter 3, we talked about how hiring is both a buying and selling process. Inexperienced managers tend to neglect this fact, forgetting that not only is the candidate selling himself to you but also that you want to convince the candidate that your company is worth working for! Once the candidate has asked his or her questions, it's time to practice your sales pitch and sell the role and the organisation. Explain the benefits and perks available when they join the company, and tell them why it's so great to work there. This is also a good opportunity to talk about what the role will entail on a daily basis. Passion and energy are infectious, and if candidates leave the interview feeling like the people who work there enjoy what they do, that will definitely give them food for thought when making their own decision. Chris Dixon, an experienced cofounder and general partner at Andreesen Horowitz, says the following about selling your company to the candidate[4]:

> *"This is the hardest part. Great programmers have tons of options, including cofounding their own company. The top thing you need to do is convince them what you hopefully already believe."*

When it comes to questions, I always encourage candidates to ask me anything about the role or the organisation. In fact, candidates who come prepared and have a few questions always score a few bonus points in my opinion! It shows that they're genuinely interested in finding out more about the company and that they're weighing their decision based on facts.

Finally, it can be helpful to explain to the candidate the next steps after the interview. How long will it take before hearing from you? Who will he or she hear from? Are there any more stages in the interview process?

Answering all these questions helps put the candidate's mind at ease and leaves them feeling good after visiting your company.

Voting

After gathering as much information as you can about the candidate, it's time to make a decision. It's a big decision because every new hire has an impact on the team. It's also important to ensure that the decision is fair and objective.

In many cases, the hiring decision is often left to the hiring manager, and while this isn't always a bad thing, it doesn't always reflect the feelings of everyone else involved in the interview. One technique that works well in this situation is to allow each person involved in the interview to give an independent hire or no-hire decision. Using a rating scale of 1 to 3, with 1 being a "yes", 2 being a "not sure", and 3 being a "no hire", you can quickly determine the general consensus in the room. And if you get everyone to reveal their number all at once, you can ensure that the interviewers don't influence each other's decision.

If you go around the room and hear mostly 1s and only a few 2s, ask each person why they gave that number. Armed with this information, you'll be able to decide as a group whether this person is a hire or not. It's also important to have a clear decision on the candidate--if there are several "nos" (3) in the room, it's a no hire immediately. Similarly, if there are too many "not sures" (2) in the room, this is a clear sign that the person isn't right for your organisation. I've found that this technique is a great way to efficiently make a hiring decision.

Google uses a another technique known as the "hiring packet", a template standardised across the company that contains notes on the candidate from every person who interviewed him or her and a score that each interviewer gives at the time of the interview. The decision on whether the candidate should be hired is based solely on a committee decision that's unbiased and includes the opinions of more than one person. In the book *How Google Works*, Eric Schmidt gives the following details about the "hiring packet"[5]:

> *"When completed, the ideal hiring packet is stuffed to the brim with data, not opinion, and this distinction is critical. If you are a hiring manager or one of the interviewers, it isn't sufficient to express an opinion; you need to support it with data."*

A great thing about this technique is that it allows you to come to a rational hiring decision based purely on facts. By giving each interviewer the opportunity to document as much information as he or she can about the candidate and to vote, you start building a clear idea of whether the candidate is right for your organisation. After all, the last thing you want is a series of clones who all share the opinions of one person!

Whichever method you decide to use, remember that everyone on the hiring team will have to work with this person. In chapter 2, we talked about culture and how each and every hire can ultimately affect it. If a few people on the team are able to give a valid reason as to why you shouldn't hire someone, it's almost definitely not worth hiring the candidate, even if that person shone in all other parts of the interview.

What to look out for in a candidate

In his book, *Smart and Gets Things Done*, Joel Spolsky says there are only two things that you need to look for in a candidate: people who are smart, and people who get things done. I couldn't agree with him more. It's easy to hire people who are extremely smart but aren't necessarily able to get things done within a given time frame. It's also easy to hire people who get things done but aren't very smart. Neither of these is a winning combination, but when you find someone who has both of these qualities, you've found a winner. The different stages of the interview are designed to help you answer whether you've found someone who has that winning combo.

When candidates submit an application for a job role, a key thing that I look for is passion and love for what they do. Earlier in the chapter, we talked about how you should look out for side projects and things done outside of normal working hours. During the on-site interview, I also look for this passion when I'm with the candidate face to face. When she talks about what she does, is there a smile on her face, is she excited? Or does it appear as if she couldn't care less about the role? In a startup, you need passionate, smart people who get things done surrounding you every day for the business to truly be successful.

In its first few years, a startup will constantly evolve and face massive change. The people who have a growth mindset with the ability to learn and adapt at every corner are the kind of people you need by your side. Candidates who are specialists in a particular area may be a great asset for a particular growth stage in your organisation, but as you grow, will they be able to adapt and learn new skills easily and quickly? These are all questions you should be asking yourself as you decide on whether a candidate is right for the role.

On the flip side, there are several things that you should look out for during the interview that are definite no-hire indicators. At the very top of the list is lying. If at any stage of the interview you're aware that a candidate has grossly exaggerated career history or perhaps given you a statement that you know to be untrue, it's almost immediately a no hire. Mistakes can happen and sometimes miscommunication is to blame, but there will be times when you can tell the difference between miscommunication and a lie. Be very wary of this.

A few years ago, I interviewed a candidate who seemed to have great potential. That is, until I touched on the reason why he was leaving his current company. At this point, he proceeded to spew fire for 10 minutes about why he hated the company and the faults of each of his managers. Needless to say, he didn't get the job! When you ask candidates about why they're looking to leave their current job, it's very likely that they have a few reasons or else they wouldn't be interviewing with you! However, if a potential candidate expresses open disgust during an interview, this isn't a good sign. Candidates in such a state rarely understand what they want. Their only goal is to get out of the situation they're in, which means they aren't in the right frame of mind. This almost always means they aren't right for your organisation at this given time. Remember: one day, it could be your company that they're spreading hate about.

Another important area to look out for is a candidate's ability to communicate. In the modern world of startups, employees must communicate and work together in teams. During the interview, I constantly ask myself if the candidate in front of me will be able to communicate effectively in a team. If there's a language barrier, or perhaps the candidate is extremely shy, if this person is working on a team, can he or she convey a point? If you can immediately answer that question with "no", there's almost no point in hiring that person.

I'm going to throw one more thing into the mix--humility. People who are humble are the easiest people to work with. They tend to be quick learners because they're willing to listen and learn from others. They don't seek credit for their work all the time, and jealously is non-existent. MailChimp's user experience director and author of *Designing for Emotion*, has the following to say about hiring for humility[6]:

> *"Humble people make great teammates. A candidate's humility, or lack of it, comes through in a longer interview process. When they checked in, how did they treat the people at the front desk? Did they ask a lot of questions? Did they take the time to learn about the company, you, and your team before the interview?"*

It's not that easy to immediately spot and hire for humility, but by ensuring that you test for soft skills and use a longer interview process, it will quickly become apparent.

Don't be a jerk

In earlier chapters, we discussed the idea that the candidate should be treated like a customer. It's a small world out there, and even if the candidate isn't right for the role, you could always convert them into an advocate for your product. I like to live by a simple rule when it comes to interviewing; don't be a jerk! Or as my good friend Robin Osborne likes to put it more forcefully: *"don't be a douche"*. It might seem silly, but the truth is that this mantra should be applied to all dealings with any candidates.

As a hiring manager, it's your role to make the hiring process as enjoyable as possible for everyone involved, especially the candidate. Remember that during on-site interviews, the candidate will be watching you and your team closely for any indicators as to what working with you will be like. Every action that you perform, whether good or bad, will help the candidate form an opinion of what your organisation is like to work for. Your body language is capable of expressing a thousand things, and it's important to keep this in mind.

When candidates visit your office for the first time, it's very likely that they'll be a little nervous. Try making them feel at ease from the minute they arrive. When you're questioning candidates during the interview process, there may be moments when they don't know the answer to a question immediately. Sometimes they need the time to think. Give it to them--moments of silence in an interview are okay! I've been in interviews where the inexperienced hiring manager just talked and talked, not giving the candidate a minute to get an answer across. If you give the candidate a few seconds to answer a question, you'll often learn vital pieces of information that otherwise would be lost in the candidate's thought process.

As candidates answer your questions, use nonverbal cues to support them. One such cue is a simple nod of the head, which can be a great way to show that you're listening. Any form of encouragement will bring the best out of the candidate during the interview. Without grinning like the Cheshire Cat, smiling is another nonverbal cue that will encourage the candidate. It's important to remember that every person who walks through the door will have different levels of confidence. Some people might be extremely shy or introverted, and it's important to keep this in mind when you interview for different roles.

Keep your bias to yourself, and give the person a chance. Just because you don't like a person's clothes or hair is no reason why you should judge a book by its cover!

By sticking to the mantra *"don't be a jerk"* you'll find that it's easy to treat candidates in the same way that you would expect to be treated. By treating the candidate like a customer, you'll ensure that your organisation starts to build a reputation as a place where people *really* want to work.

Summary

- By having a distinct set of phases for the interview process, you'll find it easier to plan, train new employees, and scale the interview process going forward.
- Before meeting with the candidate, it's important to ensure that everyone involved in the hiring is on the same page. Interview training and preparation are a great way to ensure this.
- It's important to test whether the candidate has the technical ability to perform the job on a daily basis. Working together on a simple pair programming exercise is a great way to test technical skills.
- Remember to sell your company to the candidate at the end of the interview.
- The ability for employees to communicate and work together in teams is vital, look for these traits when hiring a new employee. A candidate with only expert technical skills is not enough to work well in a team; you need emotional intelligence, too, plus humility and the ability to communicate.
- When it comes to interviews, remember the mantra "don't be a jerk"!

References

1. Joel on Software - The Guerrilla Guide to Interviewing - http://www.joelonsoftware.com/articles/GuerrillaInterviewing3.html
2. Extreme Programming - Pair Programming - http://www.extremeprogramming.org/rules/pair.html
3. How Google Works - Eric Schmidt – 2014
4. Chris Dixon - Recruiting Programmers to your Startup - http://cdixon.org/2011/12/29/recruiting-programmers-to-your-startup/
5. How Google Works - Eric Schmidt – 2014
6. MailChimp blog - Hire People not Skills - https://blog.mailchimp.com/hire-people-not-skills/

Part Three
Selecting

Chapter 7 - What Happens Next?

Congratulations! You've successfully attracted, interviewed, and selected a great candidate for your company--what happens next? You've spent untold hours in the build up to the interview process, so the last thing you want to do is lose them before they come up to speed. In this chapter we'll cover some of the techniques that startups are using to ensure that they don't lose candidates at the final stage of the interview process. We'll dive into why the first month on the job is so important, and we'll walk through the onboarding process to create one that will improve your new hire's chance of success. It's important to get these next steps right!

Adding the finishing touches

Once you've selected a candidate that you and your team feel is right for the role, you'll want to follow through with the same professionalism that you used throughout the interview process. I've seen many instances where a candidate accepts a role verbally, only to turn it down just a few weeks before the start date. There can be many reasons for why this happens--maybe the candidate changed his or her mind about the role, received a better offer from somewhere else, got the dreaded counteroffer, or had a simple personal circumstance arise. It might seem rare, but it actually happens more often than you think.

It can be a deflating and disappointing experience for everyone involved. The unfortunate truth is that this is going to happen from time to time, but by putting a few steps in place, you can ensure it doesn't happen regularly. According to the Human Capital Institute an estimated 70% of new hires make the decision to stay or leave within their first six months[1]. That is a staggering number, and it's worth thinking about how to avoid it!

Throughout this book, we've continually referred to the four key stages of the recruitment process: Planning, Attracting, Selecting, and Retaining.

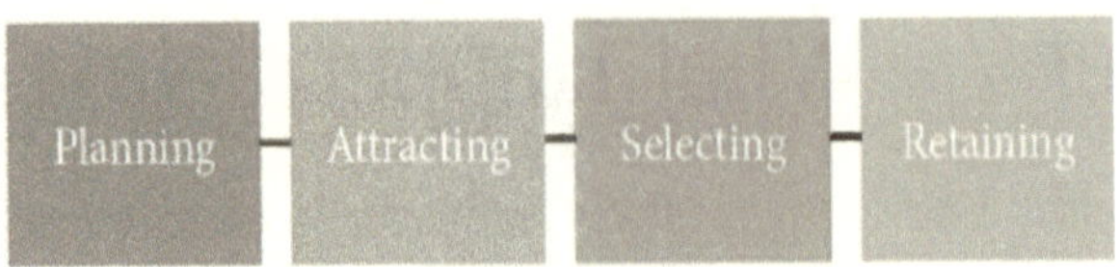

The four key stages of the recruitment process.

We'll focus here on the retaining phase. **Oddly enough, it starts sooner than** you think--the minute that an employee first joins your company!

Move quickly

If a candidate has verbally accepted the **role, get a working contract over to** them as soon as possible. Assume that the candidate is interviewing with other companies, too, so getting the contract over will reassure the person that you're making the employment official and emphasise the urgency. Imagine being eager to find a new role--having the official contract in your hand can be reassuring.

The first day joining a new company often feels like the first day at a new school; there are loads of new people to meet and an element of uncertainty involved. When you send out the employment contract, send some information letting the person know what to expect on his or her first day and week at your company. Things such as what to expect during the onboarding process can help alleviate any anxiety for the new hire.

Check in

About a week after candidates have formally accepted the role, I like to send an email welcoming them onto the team. Some organisations take this a step further and get the CEO to send new employees an email personally welcoming them into the organisation. Regardless of the size of your company, it only takes a few minutes and can be a great way to get the candidate excited about the upcoming role.

Some organisations have a longer notice period with certain roles. It isn't uncommon for more senior employees to have three-month notice periods. Try to do a quick check-in with candidates during this notice period.

Something as simple as an email saying "hello" and how excited you are to have them join goes a long way. Imagine how it must feel for a candidate not to hear anything from your organisation for such a long time. It would make me wonder if I still had a job to go to!

Send out some gear

Many startups are starting to realise that branding plays an important role in the recruitment process. Startups such as GitHub and Stripe have websites that actually sell branded clothing and products to the public. What a cool way to promote your brand and encourage employees to join your organisation at the same time!

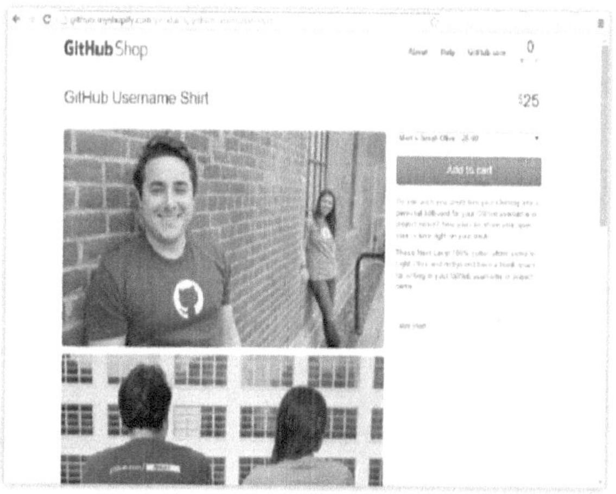

Github sell branded products to the public to promote and spread awareness about their brand.

Items such as branded t-shirts, hats, and stickers are just a few examples of some of the things that you can give away. It's a great opportunity to get creative and really get people excited. While everyone loves free stuff, it's also a good way to make people feel like part of the team right from day one. The items that you give away don't have to be expensive, but the small gesture means a lot to new starters.

Instead of giving the free gear away during the onboarding process, I prefer to present it to candidates who have formally accepted a role. If you're going to give them branded gear, send it to their home address shortly after you send out the employment contract. Scott Weiss, a partner at Venture

Capitalist firm Andreessen Horowitz, likes to call this the "welcome basket"[2]:

> *"We would put together an awesome basket of swag: t-shirts, coffee mugs, hats, Nerf guns, fruit, wine, chocolate and a handwritten note to let them know how excited we were to have them join. We'd deliver it to their home a few days after acceptance and we'd always get a shockingly enthusiastic email or phone response: 'Wow—totally unexpected!'"*

Throughout this book, we've been discussing the concept of treating candidates, and new employees, as customers. We want to delight newly hired employees and get them pumped up about working at our company. If you're thinking that the concept of a "welcome basket" is a lot of effort to put in, you're right; but remember that it can go a long way toward making a great impression right from the start. Compared to the cost of the recruitment process, giving away swag costs nothing.

Counteroffers are a common occurrence in the world of startups. Employers want to hold onto their best staff and sometimes offer an astronomical salary increase to get them to stay. While it won't always work out, by going the extra mile in the early stages you can often make someone seriously reconsider that counteroffer.

Get them involved earlier

If you have an upcoming office party or event, consider inviting the newly hired employee to join in. Even if their start date is still a few weeks away, inviting them to join in an event allows them to meet more people on the team and familiarise themselves before the big day. If the new employee has a chance to meet with the team in a relaxed, friendly environment prior to the start date, it can help alleviate those first-day nerves.

If there aren't any upcoming company-wide events, arrange a chance for new employees and the team to get together. A quick coffee or a meal out gives them the opportunity to learn about the team and help them know that they've made the right choice. As a new employee facing that first day, you can imagine that knowing a few faces can make that dreaded feeling of being the newbie a little bit more tolerable!

The importance of the first month

As we've progressed through every stage of the interview process, our goal has been to create a great experience for the candidate. Once the successful candidate joins your company, the first month should be no different. This is where a stellar onboarding process comes in.

Now that you've focused your energy on hiring the best talent, it's time to set them loose and allow them to realise their potential within your organisation. New starters can quickly align with the culture and goals of a company if given the chance to do so from the first few weeks of joining. With a great onboarding process in place your new hire will have a reduced learning curve thanks to proper training, a buddy system, and the correct equipment from the very first day. You'll notice that your new hires will become effective, contributing members of the team much quicker.

You may have seen the film *The Internship*, a comedy about two salesmen with no knowledge of modern technology who somehow find themselves getting a coveted internship at Google. While this is a fictional film, the concept is based on what really happens at Google for employees during their first few weeks. All new hires go through an onboarding program and are known as "Nooglers". It helps them learn about the culture at Google and speeds up their ability to become effective within the organisation.

Modern technology companies are realising that the transition phase for a new employee plays a vital role in setting them up for success in your organisation. Regardless of whether you're a small startup or a large organisation, new hires need to be nurtured during their first few weeks for them to hit the ground running. As we progress through the rest of this chapter, we'll explore the different techniques that you can use to set your new hires up for success.

The onboarding process

One of the best ways for new hires to learn about your organisation is through the onboarding process. Many companies will have a different approach to it, and the length of the process may also differ, depending on company size. However you approach the process, it gives you the perfect opportunity to continue from a great hiring experience into an even better first month.

Regardless of whether you choose to spread the onboarding process over one day or many, it should cover a few basic things, such as strategy, formal structures, and who to go to under different circumstances. But a good onboarding process is also capable of showing the new hire so much more. As well as being informative, an onboarding process should be fun. Sitting in HR meetings all day long is tough on anyone--get creative where possible. Rackspace, a managed cloud computing company based in the US, spends a few days of the onboarding process on games, skits, and ice-breakers. Before your next hire starts ask yourself what that person needs to be successful. Ask your current employees what they wish they had known sooner and adapt your onboarding process accordingly.

To get a better understanding of the *whole* business, have the new hire spend time with a different leader from each department each day. It doesn't have to be a lengthy meeting, but rather a chance for each leader to proudly talk about what his or her department and team work on. By getting the chance to connect socially, your new hire will better understand the culture and politics of your organisation. If you have a lot of departments, or perhaps your workforce is split across continents, stick to a handful of leaders instead. Another great technique used by busy startups is to record a video interview with team members who may be located around the world. This way, regardless of time zones and hectic meetings, your new hire will be able to learn about what each area of your business does.

In earlier chapters, we talked about the importance of hiring for cultural fit. The onboarding process is the perfect time to continue this and align the new hire with the culture of your organisation. What is your company all about? What's important to its success? Remember the saying *"culture eats strategy for breakfast"*? It means that as your organisation begins to grow and scale, strategy will only get you so far, but culture will create a meaningful purpose and bond your teams together to fight through the tough times.

Not only does onboarding help employees, but companies will reap the rewards, too. If the process is done correctly, it will boost the new hire's productivity, which in turn increases his or her overall morale. It may seem obvious, but increased morale lowers the chance of the new employee leaving shortly after joining.

The correct equipment

As an organisation, you should aim to ensure that every new hire is able to get up to speed as quickly as possible. Ensuring that new hires have all the tools at their disposal to perform their job to the best of their ability is an important part in accelerating their learning.

Simple things such as a computer with basic account settings, a corporate email account, and relevant ID cards go a long way toward helping an employee get up to speed right from day one. Not to mention the fact that it will help that person feel valued knowing that you've been preparing for his or her arrival. I can't tell you how many times I've seen organisations fail at this. If you're an employee who arrives to no basic equipment, it can be pretty discouraging.

You could even take this a step further and document all the software that employees will need to install to get started with their work. Many organisations will even pre-install software onto computers before employees arrive. More niche roles, such as software developers, QAs, or data scientists, will often require specialised software. Ensuring that you have the relevant software licences and a list of requirements will save a lot of time.

Building a list of FAQs

Regardless of whether they're toughened veterans or raw newbies, employees always have common questions. A useful way to allow them to easily access this information is to create a list of frequently asked questions (FAQs). Add them to the company intranet or even give employees a copy when they first join to serve as a useful reminder.

A computer games company called Valve Software is famous for producing titles such as Half-Life and Counter-Strike. Its games have sold over 35 million copies, and sales are constantly growing[3]. On their first day, each and every employee gets a copy of the company "handbook", which helps explain what the organisation is all about, who to go to with issues, and what projects to work on. In fact, the company has taken this a step further and made the handbook available publicly on its careers website for anyone to download4:

In the early stages of a startup, you might not have enough information to fill an entire handbook, but a collection of some of your most common questions and answers will be a great help to employees.

Get a buddy

Finding the best spots to go for lunch, determining how to order office supplies, and knowing who to ask about a specific issue are all important questions, especially if you're a new hire during your first week. While some of the answers might not belong in a list of official FAQs, they're the kind of questions that someone with local experience will be best placed to answer. Assign each new employee a "buddy" that the newcomer can comfortably ask questions no matter how trivial.

Every new team member, regardless of previous experience, should be assigned a buddy. With the help of buddies, new hires can learn the lay of the land and some of the finer details of how the organisation works. Some companies will purposefully assign buddies from another team or department. This serves as a great way for the new hire to meet new people outside of the team and widen his or her sphere of influence. However, assigning someone in the same team also works really well if you're trying to reduce the learning curve.

It's up to you to decide how long the buddy should be assigned to new hires. Many organisations aim for a full month, but I prefer to stick to a week. It's important that the new employee doesn't become too reliant on the buddy and is able to grow on his or her own. As a hiring manager, I check in with the buddy every now and then to get feedback and to find out how the new hire is progressing.

Grab lunch or a coffee

On your first day or week at a new organisation, you might not get the chance to meet everyone you'll be working closely with. If budget permits, get the team together and take them out for lunch with the new employee. It's easier to relax and enjoy the company of your new team in a casual environment.

If you prefer to keep things a bit more low key, give the buddy an allowance to take the new hire for lunch or coffee. It's another chance to break the ice and learn more about the finer subtleties of your organisation.

Creating a new employee questionnaire

Another great way to introduce new employees to the company is to use a questionnaire. For example, you could create a standard list of questions that asks the employee a little bit about him- or herself, almost like a short magazine interview. Some questions might include,

- What are you currently reading?
- What did you do at your last company?
- What would be your ideal Sunday?
- What are you currently listening to?
- What is your favorite TV show?

While these types of questions might seem a bit silly, they can be a fun excuse for employees to chat to each other and introduce themselves. Once they've completed the questionnaire, distribute it to the rest of the organisation. I've even seen some companies take this a step further and publish answers to their public website!

Putting it all together

We've covered a lot of ground in this chapter, discussing why it's so important that the first few weeks that an employee spends at your company are well-organised ones. This is an early opportunity to show that you're the same company you said you were throughout the hiring process. By delivering an impressive experience from day one, you'll ensure that your new hire is engaged and excited right from the start.

As we've learned throughout this chapter, several steps can help you ensure that your new employee has a smooth transition. The table below gives a rough guideline of the order of events and their corresponding actions.

Events	Result
Employee verbally accepts role	• Contract is sent to the new employee • Hiring manager sends out a "welcome" email
Employee signs contract	• "Welcome basket" containing swag is posted to the new employee
A few weeks before start date	• New employee invited to company-wide events to meet the team • The correct equipment (computer, software, etc.) has been ordered and will be ready on time
A week before start date	• Email to new employee about what to expect on the first day, what time to arrive, and who to ask for
The first day	• New employee attends onboarding meetings • Employee is assigned a "buddy" • All equipment is ready and prepared
The first week	• Employee goes for lunch or coffee with the team • Hiring manager checks in on employee • Employee receives questionnaire
The first month	• Team continues giving employee attention and care

As you can see, even once the employee has accepted a role at your company, there's still a lot of work involved. Dealing with people isn't as simple as a signed contract. The truth is that most companies don't have a tested, repeatable process in place for hiring and onboarding new employees, which is why paying close attention to the whole hiring process can really make a difference when it comes to Attracting, Recruiting, and Retaining talent.

By ensuring that you "wow" new employees from the first minute they come into contact with your company, you'll find that you employ eager people who are passionate about your company. In return, your new employees will feel more prepared and confident during their first few months with you. It's a win-win situation for everyone!

Summary

- Once the candidate has verbally accepted the role, move quickly and get a copy of the contract over as soon as possible.
- Check in regularly with new hires during the transition phase. Delivering a "welcome basket" can be a great way to keep your organisation in the forefront of their minds.
- If you have any upcoming company-wide events, get the new hire to come along before the first day. It's a great way to introduce the team and give the person a softer landing on day one.
- Onboarding gives the employee the opportunity to learn more about your organisation, align with your culture, and feel confident and prepared in the first few months.
- Ensure that your new hire has the correct equipment to do the job from day one.
- Assigning a new employee with a "buddy" and taking the person to lunch go a long way toward helping newbies feel like part of the team.
- Draw up an action plan for all new employees during their first week and train managers on your onboarding process.

References

1. HCI Research - The Trifecta of Engagement - http://www.achievers.com/system/files/resource/achievers-analyst-insights-theTrifectaofEngagement_Final.pdf
2. Scott Weiss - Guerilla Recruiting - Combating the Counteroffer - http://scott.a16z.com/2012/06/04/guerilla-recruiting-combating-the-counteroffer
3. Shacknews - Valve reveals lifetime retail sales - http://www.shacknews.com/article/56193/valve-reveals-lifetime-retail-sales
4. Valve Software - Jobs - http://www.valvesoftware.com/jobs

Chapter 8 - Improving the Process

Regardless of the size of your organisation, your goal should be to consistently and repeatedly hire the right people for your team. Whether you've just closed a gigantic round of hiring or employed one new person, the techniques we discussed in earlier chapters will have helped you collect vital information about your hiring process. With the right amount of analysis, this information can be used to identify areas that need improvement. After all, we want to create a successful, repeatable process for hiring great talent.

Creating a feedback loop

As I've said throughout this book, each stage of the interview process brings with it a new opportunity to learn and improve. In fact, I like to think of the process as being in a state of continuous improvement.

This is where a feedback loop comes in. In it's simplest form, a feedback loop is a way that we can constantly improve and update each stage of a process. A feedback loop occurs when a change in something ultimately comes back to cause a further change in the same thing. Feedback loops help us to learn and improve through trial and error. To visualise how this might work to help you improve your hiring process, imagine the simple feedback loop below.

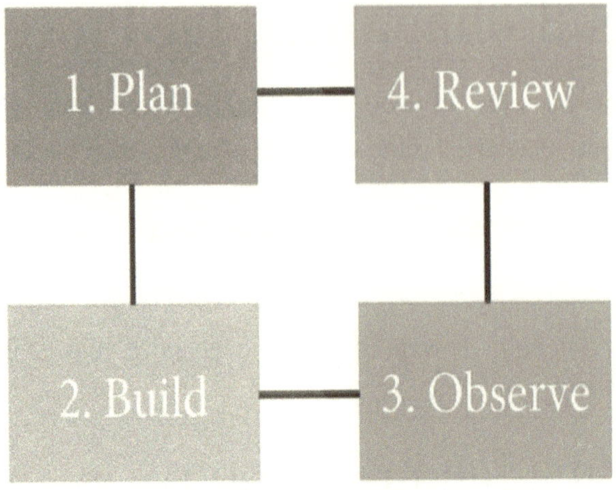

A feedback loop is an effective way to introduce change in your hiring process.

The feedback loop is broken down into four steps:

1. You start by planning the basic hiring process using the techniques that we discussed in chapters 1 to 2 of this book.
2. Once your plan is in place, you begin to build your hiring process using the techniques in chapters 3 to 6.
3. Next, you observe and track the performance of your hiring process.
4. Finally, using the data collected, you review and develop plans to update areas of the hiring process that need improvement.

The feedback loop acts as a guide that can be applied to any hiring process, regardless of the size of your organisation, to help you build a scalable, repeatable hiring process. A startup rarely stays the same for very long--over time it will grow or shrink as it responds to changes in the market. The best part about the feedback loop is that you can review it at any time and it can be a useful guide to refer back to in the future if you get stuck or are unsure of the next step in the cycle.

Three metrics every hiring manager should care about

New candidates give you and your hiring team the chance to improve your hiring skills as well as to collect vital information about your overall hiring success. There are many useful metrics that you can use to help identify areas of success or areas that need improvement. As the saying goes,

"You can't improve what you don't measure!"

Over time, you'll start to develop your own useful metrics, but a few are key to any good hiring process. As we progress through this chapter, we'll take a closer look at them.

Where did your leads come from?

Knowing where your leads came from is a fundamental metric to the success of your hiring process. Throughout this book, we've discussed the theme of treating potential candidates in the same way that we would treat customers. Regardless of whether you use online or offline methods to encourage candidates to get in touch, knowing where you're most successful will help you focus your energy.

For example, if you use your company website to promote available positions within your organisation, it's vital that you track how those candidates arrived at your website. In chapter 3, we discussed a few of the web analytics tools that you can use for this. By installing tracking snippets and using tools such as Google Analytics or Mixpanel, you'll be able to assess how people come to your site and which channels deliver the best results.

The best part about using web analytics tools is that they allow you to quickly and easily see how people are finding out about your careers website. Perhaps your Twitter account is generating a lot of interest? Or maybe people are simply finding your careers website via search engines?

Whether you're an established business or an early stage startup, you want to be able to focus your energy on the efforts that bring you the most success. If you don't intelligently target your recruiting where it works best but instead aim wildly at every channel, you'll quickly discover that recruiting can become an expensive endeavour.

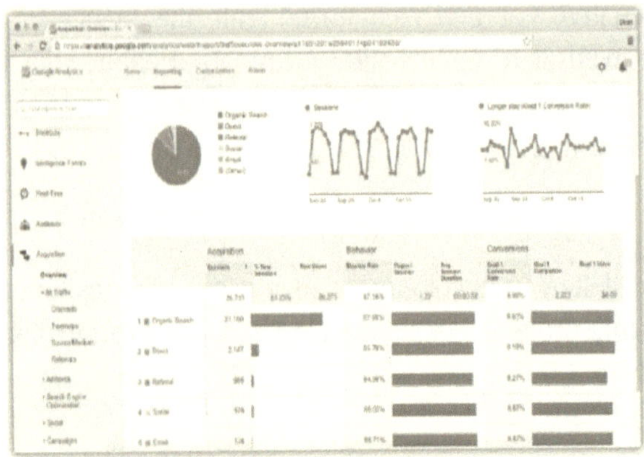

Web analytics products such as Google Analytics help track and measure where your visitors are coming from. Source: google.com/analytics

In chapter 3, we discussed the many different techniques that you can use to help drive your inbound recruiting efforts. Reaching out to potential candidates doesn't have to only involve online methods. Social connections, friends, corporate events, and even graduate fairs can be great sources of candidates for your recruitment pipeline. It can be useful to track where potential candidates may have found out about certain roles within your organisation, especially if they have come from offline sources. It can be very encouraging to know that your offline recruitment efforts are worthwhile.

As well as web analytics tools, many useful software packages can help you track and maintain your recruitment pipeline. These software packages allow you to post job openings, manage candidates, and use this data to make informed decisions. Some of the more well-known startups that offer great recruitment software are *workable.com* and *recruiterbox.com*.

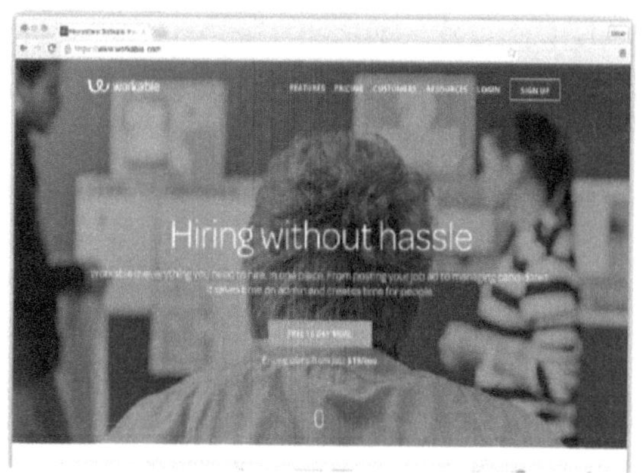

Recruitment software can be really helpful for hiring managers to track and understand where their leads come from. Source: workable.com

If, on the other hand, you prefer a more low-tech approach, you can easily build a basic solution using just a spreadsheet. If you keep a record of your leads and collate the data, it can be easily visualised. The table below gives you an idea of what it might look like using a sample dataset.

	Social Media	Careers Website	Internal Referral	Event
Account Manager	0	1	1	6
Product Manager	2	10	1	1
Software Engineer	2	1	9	0

A simple table that shows the source of interested candidates for a particular role.

If we scan the table, we can see that internal referrals worked best for the Software Engineer role, while the careers website wasn't effective at all, yet the careers website seemed to work really well for the Product Manager role.

Without this simple information at hand, it can be difficult for you to make an informed, confident decision. In a busy startup, time is a precious commodity, and misdirecting your efforts can be a waste of time. If you're an early stage startup, spending money on external recruiters can be a costly affair. If you plan to source and hire the candidates yourself during these early stages, understanding where your leads are coming from will save both time and money.

At what stage of the interview process did most of your candidates fail?

In chapter 5, we covered how the recruitment funnel allows you to easily identify how many candidates you currently have in your recruitment funnel and the stage that they're in. To get the most out of your interview process, I recommend taking it a step further and tracking where candidates dropped off at each point during the process. You can track this as a separate spreadsheet, or if you prefer, leave it to the recruiting software we covered earlier. To give a basic idea of how it might look, see the table below.

	Total	Review	Recruiter Phone Interview	Technical Phone Interview	On-Site (Technical Interview)	On-Site (Soft Skills)	Offer Accepted
Product Manager	30	6	2	1	15	5	1

Keep track of where each candidate drops off during the hiring process as it can help you pinpoint where you might need to improve.

The table contains example data for a Product Manager role. On the left, you can see that a total of 30 candidates applied for the role, and on the far right, only one candidate was accepted. Scattered through the rest of the table are the different stages at which each candidate dropped off and the corresponding numbers. The information here can be a useful tool for pinpointing exactly where you might want to improve.

For example, the number of candidates in the pipeline looks quite healthy, but one number is considerably higher than the rest. Compared to the other stages, the "On-Site (Technical Interview)" stage stands out. There could be a number of reasons why this number is higher than the rest, ranging from a poor telephone interview process to an on-site test that doesn't match the requirements for the role. The beauty of tracking this information is that it serves as an early warning signal and allows us to dig a bit deeper if necessary.

Although it's important to keep an eye on where most of the candidates dropped out during your interview process, don't let it play a major role in your decision making. Rather, use it to gauge potential issues if they do arise. In many cases, the higher dropoffs might not mean anything, but if you spot a trend across all of the roles that you were hiring for, it's worth investigating.

What was the quality of your hires?

As we know, the hiring process is split into four key stages: Planning, Attracting, Selecting, and Retaining. The two metrics that we've discussed in this chapter focus on the attracting and selecting stages of the interview process, but as hiring managers, we also want to focus on the retaining stage. You and your hiring team will have put a lot of precious time and effort into hiring great talent, and it's important to ensure that your efforts aren't in vain--especially if you're trying to build a repeatable process. Once a candidate has successfully accepted a role within your organisation, remember that the hiring process doesn't stop there. How did the new hire perform *after* he or she joined your company?

Knowing the quality of your hires is an important metric to understand. For example, if you hire 10 new employees who seem brilliant during the interview process, only to find out six months down the line that 5 have resigned in their first three months and 2 more had to be fired, this is clearly a problem! When you're hiring to fill a lot of roles in a short period of time, it's not always easy to get the quality right.

There are a number of ways to track this metric, and many companies have their own methods for doing so. It's important to determine what works best for you, but when it comes to quality of hire I like to stick to using retention rates as a measurement. The best part about this data is that it can be easily obtained from sources around you. For example, if you look closely at the retention rates within an organisation, you'll see that they can be determined by looking at the percentage of new hires who are still employed at predetermined points in time. By turning that number into a simple metric, you can calculate the average voluntary turnover rate of new hires within six months of starting (by position) compared to the average voluntary turnover rate of new hires in total from the last year.

While the quality of hire metric might seem quite simple, you can extend it as far as you want. Some organisations include manager and employee satisfaction as another measurement on top of retention rates. It's really up to you as to how far you want to extend this metric. As a hiring manager, knowing that the candidates you hire go on to become effective members of the organisation is very satisfying.

Retrospective meetings

The best form of feedback you can get often lies within your own teams. Once a round of hiring has completed, I like to get the hiring team involved in a short meeting to look back at the process as a whole. Your team should consist of a few people who can give you valuable feedback on their experiences.

In agile software engineering, the word "retrospective"[1] is used to describe a meeting held by a project team at the end of a project or sprint. This meeting is used to discuss what was successful about the project, what could be improved, and how to incorporate the successes and improvements in future iterations or projects. Regardless of whether you work in a software engineering environment that uses agile, a retrospective meeting is a very effective way of gathering feedback.

In their simplest form, retrospective meetings involve gathering the hiring team together and looking back on your latest round of hiring. Once gathered in a room, the best tools at your disposal are simply a whiteboard and a few Post-it notes.

Retrospective meetings are an opportunity to collect feedback from the team involved in the hiring process.

I find the easiest way to conduct these meetings is to draw two columns on the whiteboard, one labelled "What went well" and one "What didn't work". From there, I dish out a handful of the Post-it notes to each person involved in the retrospective meeting, and beginning with the "What went well" column, ask each person to write down a few things they thought were useful during the hiring process. Using a new Post-it for each idea, I go around the room and ask one person at a time to stick the Post-it note to the column and explain why they thought that way. Next, I ask each person to write down thoughts for "What didn't work" and add it to the corresponding column. By the time we've gone around the room, we have a list of useful things that should be improved upon or removed from the hiring process. As a final step, before leaving the meeting, I like to assign a number of related action items to specific people.

Retrospective meetings are an extremely useful way of getting feedback and involving an entire team at the same time. Not everyone will naturally be vocal when it comes to feedback, so a retrospective meeting gives everyone a chance to express their opinions and ideas in a neutral setting. This idea can also be applied to other areas of your business and used in a process of continual improvement. If you want to learn more about retrospectives, I recommend the brilliant book, *Agile Retrospectives: Making Good Teams Great*[2]. It's full of many useful ideas on how to conduct a retrospective meeting and is a helpful reference to keep retrospective meetings fresh and fun.

The truth is that no matter how good your hiring process is, there's always room for improvement. Using a retrospective meeting gives you the opportunity to stop and reflect on both the good and bad things that took place during the latest round. The actions from the meeting will improve your chances of hiring success while building a great team at the same time.

Involve new hires

At this stage of the hiring process, you should be lucky enough to have employed a few great new hires. These fresh recruits have just gone through the hiring process and will be able to bring a new perspective that you might not initially see. Take the time to ask them more about their experience of your hiring process. What did they like? What didn't they like?

Hiring is a practice that doesn't just involve a hiring manager, it involves everyone in your organisation. Each employee plays an important role, from the first moment a candidate comes in contact with your organisation all the way through to his or her first few months on the job. Often, the best people to bring a fresh perspective to a well-established hiring process will be new hires. Involve them from the start, and you'll reap the benefits. Who knows, these people may end up interviewing other candidates sooner than you think!

What to do if things still don't add up?

During my career as a manager there have been frustrating times where, as a team, we couldn't seem to fill a role for weeks on end. No matter how much we analysed the situation, reviewed data, and questioned ourselves, filling the role proved difficult. When it comes to dealing with humans, things aren't always as simple as they may seem! I remember a few years back, our team was really struggling to fill a particular role. There was no shortage of candidates, but we couldn't quite seem to find the right fit. It wasn't that the role was particularly complex, but every time we got together to vote on a candidate, something didn't work out. The reasons ranged from technical skills to personality match, and although I knew something was wrong with the way we approached this role, I couldn't put my finger on it. To make matters worse, the hiring team proved extremely picky with the candidates that came in for face-to-face interviews.

After much deliberating, we decided to mix up the hiring team a little. We started with a set team involved in hiring, but the chemistry among the interviewers wasn't quite right, so we brought in other interviewers from different teams and changed who was involved at each stage. Believe it or not, this had an immediate effect. Within a few interviews, we found the right person for the role.

While it may seem like luck at first, sometimes a small change can go a long way toward improving your chances of hiring success. Don't be afraid to mix things up a little!

Summary

- Regardless of the size of your organisation, your goal should be to create a repeatable, scalable hiring process.
- Understanding where your leads have come from will help you focus your hiring efforts whilst saving time and money.
- Knowing at which stage candidates have dropped off will help you pinpoint areas that can be improved.
- Running a retrospective meeting with your hiring team gives you the opportunity to stop and reflect on both the good and bad things that took place during the hiring process.
- You should aim to continually improve your hiring process. The feedback loop is a useful tool to help hiring managers understand that continual fine-tuning is needed in order to create a successful, repeatable process.

References

1. Retrospective - Wikipedia - https://en.wikipedia.org/wiki/Retrospective#Software_development
2. Agile Retrospectives: Making Good Teams Great - http://www.amazon.com/Agile-Retrospectives-Making-Teams-Great/dp/0977616649

Part Four
Retaining

Chapter 9 - Happy Teams

If you've ever been lucky enough to work on a team that happily works well together, you'll know how good working in an environment like that can be. There's a real buzz, and the energy in the air is almost palpable. That's why it isn't surprising to learn that happy teams and high retention levels often go hand in hand. Up until this point, we've been focussing on the individual, but going forward, we'll switch our focus toward teams. In this chapter specifically, we'll look at the importance of teams and some of the basic guidelines that will help you build happy ones.

The importance of happy teams

Whenever I chat to my grandparents about their careers and what work was like for them, I'm always fascinated by how different things were just a few decades ago. They may be retired now, but the surprising thing is that, during their careers, my grandparents only worked for a handful of organisations. In fact, my grandfather only worked for one since World War II! It wasn't uncommon for many people to stay with the first company that they joined throughout their careers.

Fast forward to the modern world, and things are surprisingly different. Employees are rarely with an organisation longer than five years, and our resumes often span multiple pages. That's why it isn't surprising to learn that more than 25 percent of all workers in the US have been with their company less than a year and more than 33 percent less than two years[1]. Higher salaries, aggressive recruiting, and high expectations are just a few of the reasons why this number is so low. In the modern world of startups especially, true loyalty is hard to come by.

You may not expect a new hire to stay with your organisation for the next 40 years, but there's no reason why you shouldn't think like that. As we will see in this chapter, the cost of losing an employee is higher than you think. Even if you forget about the time and money invested in that person, every great hire who walks out the door takes with him or her a wealth of knowledge and a tiny piece of your culture.

Let's face it, almost every human alive today will need to spend a considerable amount of their lifetime working to earn a living. We spend such a huge part of our lives surrounded by the people we work with--we even spend more time with them than we do with our families! As an employee, I would rather come into work every day knowing that the work I do is meaningful, that my team is happy, and that I enjoy what I do. Unhappy teams, unhappy departments, and unhappy organisations are the worst places to work. Any organisation will find it hard to retain employees under those conditions.

If you browse most bookshops today, you'll find a plethora of business books written about team culture and team building. The title of this chapter is a pretty bold one, and the truth is that many authors have dedicated their lives to finding the secret to building happy, successful teams. I can't claim to know the magic formula, but I can talk about a few of the things that I've seen work. As a CEO, founder, manager, team leader, or football coach, your goal should be to create great teams because a great organisation begins there.

The cost of losing an employee

Your organisation may be a wonderful place to work, but the reality is that people will eventually leave and move on. This is inevitable due to the natural ebb and flow of human movement, but there will be times when you can do something to prevent someone from leaving. The sad part is that many organisations and managers don't realise the impact of losing an employee.

The impact doesn't stop with the loss of knowledge. A recent analysis by Oxford Economics found that it takes 28 weeks on average to bring a new hire up to speed, even with the best onboarding programme in the world, it still takes time for a new person to contribute to the team. Moreover, Oxford Economics found that the loss of an employee carries with it a financial impact of over £30,000 ($45,000)[2]. This analysis took into account both the time it takes for a new hire to become productive and all the costs associated with attracting and hiring new talent.

Let's take that number and imagine the following scenario. At Acme Corp., six employees leave over a period of one year. If we add that up, it would cost around £180,000 ($270,000) to replace them! This number doesn't even take into account the many interviews and long hours involved in hiring for those six positions again.

I've heard senior executives repeat the saying, "everyone is replaceable", and while this may be a harsh, blunt way of looking at things, it doesn't take into account the cost involved or the cultural aspect of that loss. If you've been hiring for a cultural fit as we discussed in chapter 2, the loss of an employee will bring with it things that money can't buy. There will be times when the loss of an employee will be out of your hands, but in the modern world of startups, losing employees is an expense that a fledgling company cannot afford!

Happy teams = better products

In the first chapter, we looked at one of my favourite quotes from the book The Hard Thing about Hard Things, by Ben Horowitz:

"We take care of the people, the products and the profits…in that order"

Believe it or not, it has been scientifically proven that happier workers are more productive. In a study by the University of Warwick, happier workers were found to be 12 percent more productive and unhappy workers were found to be 10 percent less productive[3]. When we apply this quote to the concept of teams, it extends so much further. The key to a great team is happiness, which is why it's no secret that if you and your team love what you do, then your product and your business will be successful. We spend such a large part of our lives surrounded by the people with whom we work-- it's vital to be happy whilst doing it.

As a hiring manager, your focus should be on creating a high-performing group of individuals who have good chemistry and who can get things done. Throughout this book, our focus has been on hiring the "right" talent for your organisation, which is an important shift from simply hiring somebody that has the skills to perform the daily job. We want team players who fit in with the culture of our organisation, who are passionate about what they do. That may sound like a tall order for a hiring manager, but it's the foundation for great teams. Once you've hired the right talent for your organisation, unleash them and ensure that they have all the tools to enable them to perform to the best of their ability. Your role as a hiring manager is to hire the right people and ensure that they're happy in their work.

As we progress through the rest of this chapter, we'll look at some of the golden rules for ensuring that you and your teams enjoy a happy working environment.

Rules to live by

The key to creating happy teams isn't contained in a magic formula. In fact, if I claimed to know the answer, I wouldn't blame you for throwing this book out the window! The truth is that happy teams won't just magically appear overnight, but there are a few things that you can do to ensure that your teams are happy and able to achieve to the best of their ability. These are some rules that I like to live by.

Schedule regular one-on-one meetings

Your employees are a great source of information, ideas, and suggestions. As a manager, I find that one of the best ways to engage and find out more about the people I work with is during one-on-one meetings. Retrospective meetings and team catchups are great ways to collectively get feedback from your teams, but there will be times when things need to be said in private.

These meetings should be informal and held in a relaxed environment. I find that the best one-on-one meetings aren't long--30 minutes or so should suffice. Depending on how the meeting goes, it could take 15 minutes or even extend past the 30 minutes--it's really up to the employee. Remember that this is a chance for the employee to get everything off their chest. As a manager, you should be doing more listening than talking.

An important part of any one-on-one meeting is trust. Much like Vegas, what happens in a one-on-one meeting should stay in that one-on-one meeting. The things said by an employee in this space are for your ears only as a manager. You need to build trust, and your employee should understand that this is a forum where they can speak freely.

Depending on whether you're dealing with an introverted or extroverted person, there will be times where you aren't quite sure what to talk about. I find the best way to tackle this is to go in armed with a few questions:

- How is your current project going?
- Who do you admire on your team?
- If you could change one thing about this company, what would it be?
- What do you like/dislike about our product?
- Do you feel challenged in your current role?

Try and schedule a one-on-one meeting with each of your direct reports every two weeks. While I realise that this might seem like a lot of work, it gives you an opportunity to get a feel for how the employee is doing as well as keeps your hand on the pulse of the organisation. If you have a large number of direct reports, it might not always be scalable to meet with each and every employee every two weeks. Work around what's achievable, but remember that these meetings should happen regularly in order for you to get the best out of them.

I find that by regularly meeting with my reports, I'm able to make slight adjustments and improvements along the way. If someone is unhappy, there's often something you can do to improve the situation. One-on-one meetings are a great opportunity to get regular feedback and improve daily life for your employees.

Don't be a jerk

In chapter 6 we talked about why it's important to treat potential candidates in the same way that you would expect to be treated. This concept extends right through to being a leader. Remember that saying, "don't be a jerk"? Some of the most brilliant people I have worked with are kind, generous, and open. You'll quickly find that by treating your employees in the same way that you'd like to be treated, your teams will become happier and enjoy coming into the office.

Another important part of this equation is not expecting your teams to do anything that you wouldn't do yourself. Far too often, managers will ask things of their employees that they wouldn't dream of doing themselves if they were in their shoes. As a leader, you need to lead from the front and set the example. Embed yourself in the teams and keep one ear to the ground. People will have certain expectations of you, and it's important that you live up to them.

My favourite example of this comes from an ancient military leader known as Æthelflæd (pronounced Aethelflaed)[4]. She was known as "Lady of the Mercians" and was a ruler of a region known as Mercia in England between 911 and 918 AD. During the height of the Viking invasion in England, she was a formidable military leader and tactician, but what's surprising is that as a commander, she insisted on leading her army during large battles. Many leaders might shirk away from this responsibility and prefer to lead from a distance, she instead chose to lead from the front even in the face of danger. There's no reason why you can't follow her example as a leader--you won't even have to face down charging Vikings!

Remember that in today's world of startups, the competition for great talent is fierce. If you don't treat your employees in the same way that you would like to be treated, they'll simply move on until they find somewhere that does. Don't be a jerk!

Avoid burnout

A big part of building long-lasting teams is protecting your people. There will be tough times that will require superhuman effort from your employees, with late hours and early mornings, but this shouldn't become the norm. It's important to find a healthy balance between challenging your staff and burning them out.

The reality is that if you continue to push your staff too hard, burnout is inevitable. The most effective startup culture isn't about long hours and continual intense work, it's about striking a balance.

Twitter's engineering SVP has an interesting view on this[5]:

"Would you run your data center at 100% utilization all the time? No. Not even 80 or 90%. But some companies expect this level of performance from their people"

I couldn't agree more with this statement. People who burn out will ultimately leave your company after only working there for a short period. Throughout this book, we've been placing an emphasis on how important the brand of your organisation is when it comes to recruiting. The last thing you need is for a few disgruntled employees to leave after a short time and spread the word that your organisation is a terrible place to work.

As a hiring manager, you should be looking to create a long-term sustainable environment for your employees. Startups are crazy, hectic places, but they don't have to become places where people burn out after only a few months. Rather, you should aim to create a balanced culture and environment, a place that helps employees grow and improves their longevity in your organisation. Remember, the cost of losing an employee is a high price to pay.

Celebrate the small things

The key to a sustainable, long-term team is to build an environment where people enjoy coming into work each day. Every team is greater than the sum of its members, and while it may be true that work and personal life are often two distinct areas, you can't deny that they will overlap. It's important to celebrate the small things in your employees' lives.

Events such as weddings and newborn babies are just a few of the "small things" that are worth celebrating. If an employee has just been married, send him or her a gift certificate to someplace useful and give the person a little more time to enjoy a honeymoon. If an employee or his or her partner have just given birth, send some flowers or something special to celebrate.

It might seem small, but a thoughtful gift like this really goes a long way to show your employees that they're valued and that the team has thought about them. Celebrate the small things, and you'll find that your employees value you for it. I've worked in many companies, and I've quickly learned that it isn't easy to find a place where you enjoy the work and you're valued at the same time. Building great teams isn't always about the money--it's the small things that make a difference.

Promote leaders, not managers

In the early days of a startup, when the company is still small, high achievers really stand out. As a founder/CEO, it's easy to look at a high-achieving employee and appreciate all the great work that he or she has done. The next thing you know, the employee goes from being a software engineer to being in charge of the team. This is the point at which problems start to arise.

This story is an all too familiar one that happens far too often in startups. People who are amazing individual contributors don't always make amazing leaders. It's important to make a clear distinction between leadership and management here. Management involves planning, budgeting, organising, and staffing; leadership involves setting direction, influencing, motivating, and enabling others to contribute to organisational success. I see a leader as someone who people will willingly follow even during the tough times. Let's face it: if you can't stand your manager, it's highly unlikely you'll stick around when times get tough. As the well-known saying goes, "people quit their boss, not their job". It can be hard enough to get great talent to stick around during the good times, and a manager that isn't a great leader may be a good reason why people are leaving your organisation.

All of this boils down to the team itself. A key part of a happy team is the respect that its members have for their leader. A leader is no greater than the sum of the parts of a team, but instead fulfills a role that should motivate, encourage, and guide the team through tough times. As soon as an individual who isn't right for the role (or gets promoted too quickly) starts to lead, team morale dips and people begin to look elsewhere. It's a pattern I've seen happen many times before. One of my favourite quotes around leadership is from the book *Debugging Teams* by Brian Fitzpatrick and Ben Collins-Sussman:

> *"Traditional managers worry about how to get things done, while leaders worry about what things to get done…(and trust their team to figure out how to do it)".*

The very best way to reduce the chances of a bad promotion is to take your time before you promote that star individual to a leadership role. It's worth asking yourself if he or she is able to perform some of the trickier aspects of the role before a promotion. Will great people want to work for him? What is her level of emotional intelligence? Could he give tough, honest feedback during a one-on-one meeting?

If you do promote someone, remember that new leaders need training and guidance themselves. Try and pair them with someone who has performed a similar role successfully for a while. It gives the new leader a chance to learn and ask tough questions that few others would be able to answer. Invest in your leaders in order to help them become great, and you'll only reap the rewards.

Drive innovation

If you work in an organisation where the majority of your day-to-day work revolves around repetitive tasks, it isn't easy to break the mold and experiment with new ideas. Many tech startups around the globe hold "hack days" or "hackathons" to give employees the chance to spread their creative wings. As a basic rule, an internal hack day is run over the period of a day (or more), with teams getting together to create something outside of their normal work. Tech companies regularly use this concept to drive innovation and experiment with new technologies. The great thing about this concept is that it doesn't just work with software engineering teams, it can work with entire companies!

Once you've established who's going to be involved in the hack day, find a suitable location with great WiFi and access to the equipment the teams will need. From there, unleash the teams and allow them to think outside the box and create something within the given time frame. Once complete, get everyone together and vote on the best project. I've never walked away from a hack day without being impressed with the great ideas that teams have come up with.

Another great concept that drives innovation is known as "20 percent time". Large companies such as Google allow their employees to spend 20 percent of their time (one day a week) working on side projects that benefit the organisation. Some of the most famous Google products are a result of this, including Instant Search, Google Now, Google News, and many more. As Eric Schmidt says[6]:

"The most valuable result of 20 percent time isn't the products and features that get created, it's the things that people learn when they try something

A key reason that many employees leave their jobs is because they don't feel challenged, or they've stopped learning. Using techniques such as hack days or 20 percent time gives your employees the chance to continually learn something new and recharge their creative batteries. If you're trying to create happy teams that are constantly learning, give your employees the chance to innovate. Who knows what will come out of the time spent on innovation!

Eat together

No matter what size organisation I've worked in, the first sign of a happy team is one that eats together. I don't just mean sitting at desks eating a sandwich and talking, but rather eating lunch in the canteen or office workbench. Humans are social creatures, and spending time together only helps strengthen the bonds between us. The informal talk that takes place when teams break bread together is a great example of what we should be promoting as leaders.

The sad thing is that in the modern office, many employees will sit at their desks and continue working while eating their lunch. Encourage your team to eat together every so often, and you'll find laughter and happiness, rather than the clicking of a keyboard and little social interaction. Many managers make the mistake of frowning upon full lunch hours--in fact, leaders should encourage it. Don't get me wrong, when it's crunch time, the team should be prepared to put in the hours, but it shouldn't be the norm to skip lunch breaks.

Eating together is a great way to build relationships among people and create a culture of trust and respect.

Give praise

If you've worked really hard on a project, it feels good to receive recognition for it. Even the humblest person appreciates being praised for hard work. Whether you're the CEO or a small team's leader, praising an employee goes further than you think. In fact, giving someone praise will actually boost morale and improve employee satisfaction. A recent study by the O.C. Tanner Institute found that 7 out of 10 employees who report they've received some form of appreciation from their supervisors say they're happy with their jobs[7].

As an employee yourself, you know it doesn't take a study to work out that receiving praise feels good. But as a manager, it's so easy to forget to praise people for a job well done. Too often, we think that monetary rewards will make someone feel valued at work. Some of the best managers I've ever had were quick to praise and reward good work. The truth is that giving employees recognition will help you engage with them, retain them, and even accelerate their performance. The best thing about it is that it's free!

Take a look around

Believe it or not, there is overwhelming evidence that office design impacts the health, well-being, and productivity of its occupants[8]. Stop and think about your office for a second--what are your first thoughts? What's the layout like? How does it make you feel?

Whether we like it or not, our environment directly affects our happiness and well-being. I've worked in some very early-stage startups where the bins were overflowing and the office was extremely untidy. I realise this is an extreme case, but as you can imagine, many people loathed spending time there. Eventually, we sorted out the teething problems, but this was a real eye opener for me!

In the early stages of a startup, money is always going to be tight. Spending money on plush offices and the latest Swedish designer furniture isn't easy to justify. I'm not saying that you need to do this, but that you should stop and consider the environment around you every now and then. It's worth reviewing:

- **Daylight and lighting** -- Does your office have enough natural lighting? Exposure to natural light has been linked to improved performance and sleep.
- **Noise** -- In most open-plan offices, noise is a common distraction. Is there anything that can be done about it?

- **Thermal comfort** -- The temperature in the office has a significant impact on workplace satisfaction. If it's summer and the temperature is sweltering inside, you're going to have a few unhappy (not to mention sleepy) employees on your hands!
- **Plants** -- A growing volume of research demonstrates the importance of greenery and the natural environment to health and well-being.

I've only touched on a few areas worth considering around your office, but it's vital to consider this when you think about the happiness of your employees.

Summary

- The cost of losing an employee is higher than you think: around £30,000 ($45,000) for each employee!
- Happy workers are more productive, and it's no surprise to learn that happy teams build better products.
- Schedule regular one-to-one meetings with the people in your teams in order to get regular feedback and improve life for your employees.
- Don't ask your teams to do anything that you wouldn't do in their shoes.
- To avoid burnout, aim to create a balanced culture and environment where employees aren't expected to work ridiculous hours.
- Individual contributors don't always make amazing leaders--be cautious before you rush into that next promotion!
- Don't forget to give your employees recognition for great work.
- The office environment directly affects the happiness and well-being of your employees. Consider reviewing it every now and then.

References

1. Employee Tenure in 2002 - BLS - http://www.bls.gov/news.release/history/tenure_09192002.txt
2. The Cost of Brain Drain - Oxford Economics - http://www.oxfordeconomics.com/my-oxford/projects/264283
3. Happiness and Productivity - Andrew J. Oswald, Eugenio Proto, and Daniel Sgroi -

https://www2.warwick.ac.uk/fac/soc/economics/staff/eproto/workingp

4. Æthelflæd - Wikipedia -
   https://en.wikipedia.org/wiki/%C3%86thelfl%C3%A6d
5. Unlocking the Power of Stable Teams - First Round Review -
   http://firstround.com/review/Twitter-Engineering-SVP-Chris-Fry-on-
   the-Power-of-Stable-Teams
6. How Google Works - Eric Schmidt – 2014

7. The Easiest Thing You Can So to Be a Great Boss - HBR.org -
   https://hbr.org/2015/11/the-easiest-thing-you-can-do-to-be-a-great-
   boss
8. World Green Building Council - Health, Wellbeing and Productivity
   in Offices -
   http://www.worldgbc.org/files/6314/1152/0821/WorldGBC__Health

Chapter 10 - Managing Talent for the Future

"What are my prospects for the future?" This is a question that almost every employee will ask themselves at some point. Smart people want to know that they're able to learn, to grow, and to have a future with your organisation. Once the excitement of being a new hire wears off, people begin to assess their long-term prospects. This is why it's so important to consider the growth of your employees. After all, if you've hired great talent, you want to ensure it flourishes. In this chapter, we'll focus on managing talent for the future.

Career path and progression

If you ask any employee in your company right now what his or her career path within your organisation looks like, can that person tell you? As an employee, it's a good feeling to know that you have a future with a company and that you can grow your career. I've come across times when employees have handed in their resignation merely because they felt they didn't have any future prospects in that particular place. This is an all too familiar theme among many companies around the world. If you hire bright, eager, passionate people, at some point they'll begin to look at the next step on the ladder...ideally, you want that ladder with you, not another company!

As a leader, you can influence employee growth and guide career paths. Employees want to feel fulfilled and find happiness in their work. Setting a career path doesn't need to be complicated--let's look at a simple one for a software developer using the image below.

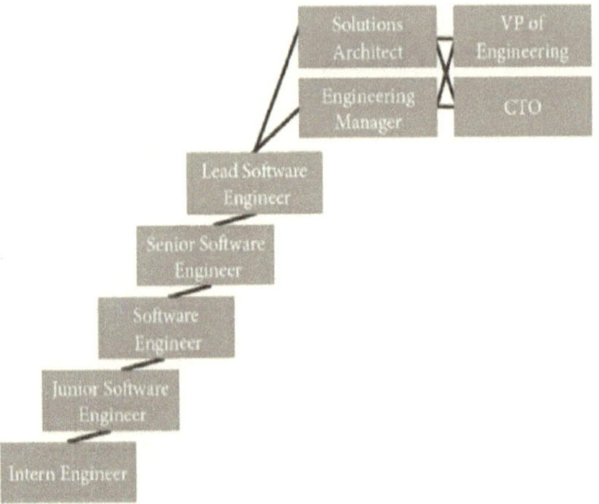

A basic career path for a Software Engineer starting from an Intern all the way to CTO at a startup.

Starting from the bottom of the image, we can see our Software Engineer starting as an Intern Engineer, but the role progresses right through to VP of Engineering or CTO depending on the route taken. Although this will differ from organisation to organisation, you can see that there are a lot of options available to an engineer joining the company. As we've discussed in earlier chapters, some people lean naturally toward a leadership role, while others might prefer a more technical one. How they progress through their career is really up to them, but options are key. Having a defined and transparent career path in place helps you grow and nurture their skills accordingly. Do they have the skills to progress to the next level? If they don't, you'll be able to guide and mentor them to help them get there.

Smart people need to feel that they can advance in their careers. Sometimes this can be more difficult in a smaller startup, especially if you don't expect to hire new people or grow much in the next few years. As a leader, you might not be able to promote your staff during this time, but there are a few other options available to you. First, don't be afraid to venture outside of a role's defined career path. Let your employees know that if there is another area of the business that interests them, they can move laterally between roles. This gives them the option to learn something new whilst challenging them at the same time.

Employees who have their intellect challenged daily won't become bored easily. Smart people don't like to live in a world of boredom or to let their skills stagnate. Provide everyone with the opportunity to learn and grow even if you might not be able to promote them.

Promotions

An important part of the career path is promotions and job titles. Regardless of the size of your organisation, having a title helps employees understand who's who and what each person does. Believe it or not, employees actually want these titles--they help your team not only internally but when they move on as well! Promotions play an important part in recognising an employee's contributions. It's a two-way street for an employer; not only will your employees feel rewarded for their hard work, but being promoted can also be a great way to push your people to take on new challenges.

At a startup, handing out promotions in the same way that a large corporation does won't always scale. If your business is small and you aren't often hiring, the urge to promote people can seem immense. I've worked in a few startups where employees had crazy titles, such as head of sales, even when they were the only salesperson in the organisation! As a manager, you might feel like you're doing the right thing and rewarding your employees by giving them great titles, but you might actually be doing them a disservice. For example, if your organisation suddenly starts to grow and you employ 30 new people in sales, will your "head of sales" be able to scale and cope with the new role? Hiring someone above this person will be tricky, and you risk either demoting or losing that person. As a CEO/founder of a startup, the promotion of each and every employee needs to be managed with care!

When it comes to promotions, it's important to be objective and fair. When I think back to the organisations where I've worked, the ones with the fairest and most obvious promotion strategies were the ones with a defined promotion process in place. As a manager, it's easy to fall into the trap of promoting an employee without clear results. Just because someone has been with you for a while, or is considering leaving, isn't a valid reason for you to promote that person. Every action that you take has a ripple effect, and you could end up alienating an entire team by making the wrong promotion.

We've all had that moment of wondering, "How on earth did that person get that role?" when referring to a colleague. This is a perfect example of the Peter Principle in action. The *Peter Principle* is a book written in 1969 by

Lawrence J. Peter, but it's still very accurate and useful today. It put forth the concept that the selection of a candidate for a promotion is based on the candidate's performance in his or her current role, rather than on abilities related to the intended one. It suggests that everyone in an organisation will keep on getting promoted until they reach their level of incompetence. At that point, they stop being promoted. Given enough time and enough promotion levels, every position in an organisation will be occupied by someone who can't do the job. That's a pretty scary thought!

But you can combat this horrible hypothetical future: by ensuring that all promotions are based on the required skills for the next stage of the role's career path, you'll guarantee that people don't get promoted into a position they can't do. When a clearly defined promotion system works well, it can be a great platform for recognising an employee's contributions and rewarding a job well done.

Training

Throughout this book, our goal has been to build an effective hiring process and a place where employees want to work. You've spent countless hours attracting, reviewing, hiring, and onboarding great talent. It's important to ensure that you keep your employees' skills sharp and up to date. Unfortunately, training is often overlooked as a useful means of retaining your staff.

I've spoken to many managers who have been cautious to invest in their employees' growth. There's a misconception that once an employee has attended a course or learned a new skill, they'll suddenly decide to leave the company. In fact, it has the exact opposite effect. Employees know that they have a future in your company and that you're willing to invest in them. Encourage them to learn and use their skills, and you'll find that you end up with a better workforce that's more engaged and satisfied.

It's true that in the early stages of a startup, money is tight, but that's no reason why you can't help your employees improve and grow their skills. There are plenty of different options that are free or cost very little, and they can go a long way toward helping employees feel valued and like they have a future with your organisation.

Online training

Investing in your employees doesn't have to cost an arm and a leg. I'm a big fan of online learning as it can be done at a convenient time with little disturbance to day-to-day work. Your employees can log on for an hour or two at a time and top-up their skills.

You'll also be surprised to know that many of these online learning platforms have access to over tens of thousands of books and videos. Thanks to modern technology, this sort of knowledge is available at our fingertips and on demand.

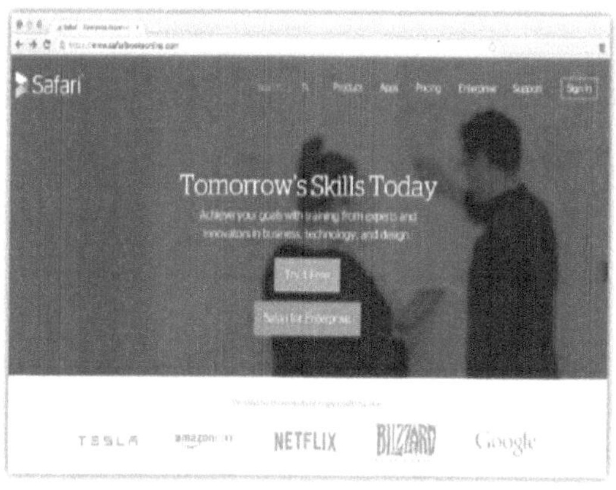

Online learning providers such as safaribooksonline.com have access to over 30,000 books and videos.

Some of my favourite online learning providers include Safari Books, Udacity.com, OReilly.com, and Pluralsight. You'll also find that many popular online learning providers also offer the occasional free course, which is a great starter to test out on your employees. At first glance, it may appear as if these providers are purely geared at tech startups, but most online learning providers will cater to a wide array of business sectors and industries. All it takes is an hour here or there every week for an employee to grow and learn new skills.

Conferences

Nothing fires me up more than attending a conference and seeing how other leading organisations are building great businesses. Conferences are a great way to engage your team and help them learn at the same time. Large conferences with speakers who are respected offer the perfect opportunity for you and your team to learn from some of the best minds out there. How often do you get to spend time in an audience with talented individuals from some of the most well-known, successful organisations in the world?

Giving your employees the chance to either attend or speak at a conference will make them feel valued and engaged. Conferences are a useful learning tool for all roles, regardless of the employee's level of experience--there's literally something for everyone.

Books

Remember those dark times before the internet? Books were the best source of knowledge and often the only way to spread new ideas to a large audience. I still believe this holds true today. In fact, so do you if you're reading this! During my career, I've noticed that different people prefer different mediums to learn something new. For example, I like reading books to expand my knowledge, while someone else might prefer to watch online videos. Give your employees different options, and you'll find that each of them will embrace learning head on!

For the price of a few dollars, a book can be a low-cost way of passing on valuable knowledge to your employees and keep them up to date with the industry trends. In some cases, the online learning providers we mentioned earlier will have an eBook option, too. However, I find the best approach is to have a shared spreadsheet that employees can update with books that they would like to read that are related to their roles. Every few months, you can then refer to the spreadsheet and place an order for the books. If you are buying for an entire department it might seem like a lot of money, when you think about the price of a book per employee, it costs a lot less than a conference or a training course!

Meetups and events

From business to social, meetups are a great way to learn from others and contribute at the same time. In chapter 3, we discussed how local meetups are a good way to stay involved in your particular market while still generating potential recruitment leads.

During my career I've been passionate about improving website performance, and I regularly attend a local meetup on this very topic. Over the years that I've been attending, I've made friends and learned so much at the same time. Other organisations might face the same everyday issues that you do, and a meetup gives a great forum to learn from their successes.

Encourage your employees to attend local meetups, and you'll be surprised by how much they learn and are able to apply to their daily work. Depending on the individual, you could even encourage them to give a talk at a local meetup. For a first-time speaker, it's a useful place to practice public speaking with a small group and teach others at the same time.

If your organisation is involved in a particular industry and there's no local meetup, consider creating one yourself. If your employees attend these events and give presentations, they can be a shining example of what it's like to work for you and the different technologies that you might use.

Lunch and Learn

In the early days of a startup, things can often seem chaotic. Time is money, and every minute that your employees are working on your product is precious, which is why it isn't always easy to spare an employee's time to attend a conference or event. On the other hand, it's vitally important to allow your employees the opportunity to grow and learn new things. Balancing these two conflicting priorities isn't easy.

I find that "Lunch and Learns" are a great way to get more training done and make the best use of a lunch hour at the same time. The simplest definition of a Lunch and Learn is that it's a training event scheduled during lunch. At this point, you might be thinking that it sounds extremely boring and it won't be easy to get people to attend. In fact, it's the exact opposite! During this hour, the training is less formal and structured--in fact, it's kind of fun. Employees can bring in their own lunch and eat it during the session, or if you have the budget for it, you could organise lunch for everyone--that's a sure-fire way to get your attendance levels up!

The most important part of a Lunch and Learn session is that it needs to be voluntary. Lunch break is an important time to many people, and they may have errands they need to run during this time. If the sessions are voluntary, people can decide for themselves whether they want to attend.

Your employees are a fantastic source of information. If someone recently attended a conference, ask that person to share with everyone what she learned--similarly, if someone read a compelling book or took an online training course, ask him to talk about the experience. If you run out of ideas for sessions, simply Google "Lunch and Learn ideas", and you'll be presented with a plethora of different options. Lunch and Learn sessions shouldn't feel forced. If no one has anything to share, simply defer to another session.

Salaries and the future

Let's face it, no matter how much we love a job, at the end of the day we all work for a salary. Some people are more driven by it than others, and it definitely isn't a motivating factor for everybody, but ultimately everyone wants to be paid their salary at the end of the month. When you strip away the passion and enjoyment that your job brings, you're left with mortgages to pay, children to feed, vacations, and the rising cost of a beer. All of these things cost money, which our salaries provide.

A well laid out career path can actually be extended further and used as a grading system for salaries. Let's look at the Software Engineer example we used earlier--it can be used to determine what the salary range might be at every stage of that particular career path. What does a Senior Software Engineer earn? What does an Intern earn? The best thing about doing this is that it creates a fair and transparent salary system. No matter how much effort is put into keeping salaries private, eventually people tend to find out what everyone else is earning. There's nothing worse than finding out that someone who joined a year after you earns a lot more.

In fact, the early stages of a startup is the perfect time to clearly define a salary grading system. If you set this out right from the start, you'll be able to set clear salary grades based on the career path thus creating an honest and transparent environment. If you pay everyone fairly, there's no reason why you can't be transparent. In fact, companies such as Buffer have even disclosed their salaries for each grade online [1]. It also has an online calculator to work out what your salary would be if you worked at Buffer[2]. It's great to see this level of transparency, but I'm not necessarily suggesting that you do the same!

An important part of considering pay grades based on a career path is promotions. When someone is promoted to the next level, it's just as important to ensure that his or her salary moves up, too. I've worked in many organisations where people are promoted, but their salaries aren't moved up, or they simply receive a measly pay rise. As amazing as the culture of your organisation might be, the reality is that people will eventually move on if they can get paid a better salary elsewhere. It's worth revisiting salaries at least once a year. If you have a set time where salaries are adjusted, instead of on an ad hoc basis, it's easier to be transparent and open about when people might receive an increase. It can also be very tempting to give someone a pay rise when they threaten to leave or are offered a role somewhere else. Counteroffers are an expensive Band-Aid and won't fix the root cause of an employee's unhappiness. It may buy you some time, but ultimately there are deeper reasons why someone considered leaving in the first place. If you find that you're constantly counter offering, you'll set a bad precedent--the last thing you want to do is create an environment where this becomes the norm. If you revisit salaries at regular intervals, you'll quickly find that your employees have a clear understanding about how their salaries work.

Equity

A common technique among many startups is to actually offer new hires equity, or stock, as a means to supplement their overall salary. If your startup is experiencing rapid growth, equity will seem like an attractive option to many interested candidates. It can also be another way to offset a lower base salary; successful startups might offer a new employee a large amount of equity that could one day become worth a large amount.

For an employee who might have never worked in a startup before, equity can be a bit confusing. When it comes to new hires, put together a bit more detail and explain to them exactly what they need to know about equity. You should be able to give them a recent valuation of your organisation along with the number of outstanding shares. Any new hire should be looking at what their equity will be worth in 2 to 5 years, not what it's worth today. I really like what Chris Dixon, a general partner at Andreessen Horowitz, says about this[3]:

> *"The only thing that matters in terms of your equity when you join a startup is what percent of the company they are giving you. If management tells you the number of shares and not the total shares outstanding, so you can't compute the percent you own -- don't join the company!"*

The reality is that many startups will fail before the equity actually becomes worth real money. The world of equity can be tricky and as an employee, it can be difficult to understand exactly where you stand. Many younger employees who have never worked for a startup can easily be lured in with the promise of equity without realising its immediate worth.

Don't get me wrong: equity is a very important part of a startup. If you've been working for a company for a long time, it's good to know that your hard work could be rewarded one day!

Summary

- Planning out a career path for every employee will help everyone understand the different options that they have with your organisation for the future.
- Regardless of the size of your organisation, having a title helps employees understand who's who and what they do in the organisation.
- Promotions can be a great way to push your team to take on new challenges.
- Don't neglect training. Help your employees improve and grow their skills, and you'll only benefit in the long run.
- Online training, conferences, books, meetups, and Lunch and Learns are useful ways to help your employees grow.
- When it comes to salary, map it to the career path for the role. It's important to be open and transparent about pay grades to create an environment of trust.
- You've put a lot of effort into each stage of the hiring process. Don't lower the bar!
- Hiring the right people for your teams will enable your organisation to soar to new heights.

References

1. Open Salaries at Buffer: Our Transparent Formula and All Our Salaries - Buffer.com - https://open.buffer.com/introducing-open-salaries-at-buffer-including-our-transparent-formula-and-all-individual-salaries
2. Buffer's Transparent Salary Calculator - buffer.com - https://buffer.com/salary
3. The Number One Thing You Should Know about Your Equity Grant - cdixon blog - http://cdixon.org/2009/08/28/the-one-number-you-should-know-about-your-equity-grant